SPIRITUAL INSIGHTS

THE LORD JESUS CHRIST

IS

THE LIGHT OF THE WORLD

EVELYN B PENNEY

BALBOA.
PRESS

A DIVISION OF HAY HOUSE

Balboa Press books may be ordered through booksellers or by contacting:

Balboa Press
A Division of Hay House
1663 Liberty Drive
Bloomington, IN 47403
www.balboapress.com
1 (877) 407-4847

Because of the dynamic nature of the Internet, any web addresses or links contained in this book may have changed since publication and may no longer be valid. The views expressed in this work are solely those of the author and do not necessarily reflect the views of the publisher, and the publisher hereby disclaims any responsibility for them.

The author of this book does not dispense medical advice or prescribe the use of any technique as a form of treatment for physical, emotional, or medical problems without the advice of a physician, either directly or indirectly. The intent of the author is only to offer information of a general nature to help you in your quest for emotional and spiritual well-being. In the event you use any of the information in this book for yourself, which is your constitutional right, the author and the publisher assume no responsibility for your actions.

Any people depicted in stock imagery provided by Thinkstock are models, and such images are being used for illustrative purposes only.
Certain stock imagery © Thinkstock.

ISBN: 978-1-4525-8295-5 (sc)
ISBN: 978-1-4525-8296-2 (e)

Printed in the United States of America.

Balboa Press rev. date: 1/3/2014

AUTHOR

EVELYN B. PENNEY

This is a collection of lessons I have learned on my pilgrimage through life. For over forty years, God has patiently shared His love with me and showed me His purpose for creating mankind in His image. The inspirations were received mostly through the Bible, which I have studied extensively in various translations of Scripture. I have also researched many commentaries and listened to sound Christian radio programs.

DEDICATED

TO

MY CHILDREN AND GRANDCHILDREN

David

Alice

John

James

The painting on the cover is the artwork of Alice

It is my fervent prayer that these insights may help my children, grandchildren and friends
to draw closer to the Savior Jesus Christ. He is the only One who has solutions
for all problems in this world. He is truly the Way, the Truth and the Life.

January 1

MORNING PRAYER

Dear heavenly Father -

I ask you to fill me with your Spirit through Jesus Christ, your Son.
Grant that today I may never be unaware of your Presence.
Help me to discern and obey your will.
Guard my mind against anything that is contrary to your nature.
Cleanse my thoughts that I may not dwell on fear, pride, criticism and self-pity.
Bridle my tongue that I may not speak any untrue, unkind and unnecessary words.
Seal my lips that I may not seek comfort in food.
Fine-tune my ears that I may hear your Still, Small Voice.
Open my eyes that I may see all the beauty you have created.
Guide my hands that I may do your work with diligence and skill.
Direct my feet that I may be at the right place at the right time.
Work in my heart that I may convey love and compassion to others.
Grant that I may begin, continue and end this day in harmony with you,

Through Jesus Christ, my Lord.   Amen.

January 2

THE TRINITY

GOD -	Sovereignty. Isaiah 45:5-7; Daniel 4:35
	Holiness. Psalm 99:9; Psalm 145:17
	Love. Jeremiah 31:3; John 3:16
CHRIST -	Sinbearer. 2 Corinthians 5:21; 1 Peter 2:24
	Advocate. 1 Timothy 2:5; 1 John 2:1
	Friend. Matthew 11:28-30; John 15:15
HOLY SPIRIT -	Teacher. John 14:26; John 16:13
	Supplier of strength. Isaiah 40:31; 1 John 4:4
	Helper. Psalm 138:7-8; Romans 8:26

God the Father, God the Son and God the Holy Spirit are all God with the same divine attributes, but distinct functions.

God's justice demanded that we pay for our sins, but His love provided the payment.

Christ willingly paid our penalty by offering His sinless life as a sacrifice.

The Holy Spirit assists us in our sanctification.

January 3

GOD'S REASONS FOR CREATING MAN

PLANTS –   have a body.
ANIMALS – have a body and a soul (instinct, will, emotions).
HUMANS – have a body, soul (mind, will, emotions) and a spirit. We are created in
*   God's image and can therefore communicate with Him.*

- We are to have an intimate relationship with God and praise Him forever.
  Jeremiah 31:3; Psalm 100
- We are given the responsibility to care for and rule over God's creation.
  Genesis 2:15; Psalm 8:6
- We are co-creators with God by putting ideas into action for His Glory.
  John 15:8; Colossians 3:17
- We are to be channels for God's love to reach others.
  Matthew 5:16; John 15:12

January 4

FELLOWSHIP WITH GOD

- Become aware of the awesomeness of God in His creation.
- Learn who God is from His Word.
- Follow the Bible as God's instruction book for your life.
- Confess and repent of your sins.
- Accept Christ's atonement for your sins.
- Commit yourself to trust, obedience and praise.
- Make a personal relationship with the Lord the center of your life.

January 5

SEPARATION FROM GOD

- Change the concept of creation to evolution.
- Invent a god to suit your philosophy.
- Reject the instruction in the Bible as God's Word.
- Rely on your own goodness to be accepted by God.
- Claim direct access to God without Christ.
- Choose personal freedom over commitments.
- Make either self or a form of religion the center of your life.

TRUTH VERSUS ERROR

TRUE - Inerrancy of the Scripture. Deuteronomy 12:32; Psalm 119:89;
Matthew 5:17-18; 24:35; 2 Peter 1:20-21; Revelation 22:18-19

FALSE - Use the Bible like a cafeteria; take what you like, leave the rest. View
the Bible as obsolete, outdated, unscientific, unreliable, a mere allegory.

TRUE - God created everything out of nothing. Gen 1:1-31; John 1:3; Colossians 1:16

FALSE - Evolution, Big Bang.

TRUE - Creation became, and still is, contaminated by evil. The second
Law of Thermodynamics. Genesis 3:1-24

FALSE - Everything is getting better. Man is born innocent.

TRUE - The Virgin birth of Jesus. Matthew 1:18-25; Luke 1:34-38
Jesus is the Son of God. Matthew 16:13-17; Luke 22:70; Rev 22:13

FALSE - Jesus is the natural son of Joseph and Mary. He was an enlightened teacher
with an advanced consciousness.

TRUE - The shedding of Christ's blood is necessary to atone for our sins.
Romans 3:24-25; 5:9; Ephesians 2:13; Hebrews 9:22;

FALSE - Self-improvement and a raised consciousness can overcome sin.

TRUE - God can only be approached through Christ. John 3:16-36;
John 14:6; Acts 4:12; Romans 5:1-2; Ephesians 2:18; 1 Timothy 2:5

FALSE - Each person has direct access to God without Christ.

TRUE - The second coming of Christ is a real event in the future.
Acts 1:11; Revelation 1:7

FALSE - The Christ consciousness in man is an ongoing process.

HOW TO RESPOND TO PROBLEMS

WRONG RESPONSES

- Accusing God or blaming Satan.
- Blaming others.
- Lashing out in anger.
- Holding anger in.
- Resignation.
- Self-pity.

RIGHT RESPONSES

- Thanking God by acknowledging His sovereignty, righteousness, love and ultimate goal for us. Ps 34:1; Ephesians 5:20; 1 Thessalonians 5:18; Romans 8:28-29
- Identifying possible causes in ourselves through introspection, confession and repentance. 1 Corinthians 11:31-32; 1 John 1:9
- Developing Christ-like qualities and attitudes. Humility, repentance, meekness, mercy, purity, peacemaking and endurance in persecution. Matthew 5:3-12
- Becoming sensitive to the needs and hurts of others. This presents an opportunity to express love and compassion. Matthew 5:44; John 13:34-35;
- Knowing that we find ourselves on a journey, beset by temporary hardships, but moving steadily towards all glory in heaven. Psalm 30:5; John 14:1-4; John 16:33; Romans 8:18; Hebrews 12:2; Revelation 21:4

A SPIRITUAL DIET

TO ABSTAIN FROM -

Bitter herbs of resentment.
  Sour pickles of unforgiveness.
    Sharp spices of gossip.
      Rich desserts of self-indulgence.
        Ego-building proteins of selfishness.
        Heavy bread of materialism.
          Bland puddings of complacency.
            Strong stimulants of criticism.
             Drugging wine of self-pity.

January 9

TEN CONVICTIONS

- God is sovereign. He is omniscient, omnipotent and omnipresent.
    He is in total control of everything.
- The Bible is God's Word and His final authority.
- My purpose in life is to seek God with all my heart, to trust Him in everything
    and to obey Him out of love and gratitude.
- I am a living witness for Him in whatever I am, say and do.
- My body is the living temple of God and must not be defiled by the lusts of the world.
- My affections must be set on things above, not on things of the earth.
- Everything I have is God's property. I am the caretaker and steward, responsible for the management.
- Forgiveness by God through the shed blood of Jesus Christ can only be received
    when I confess, repent and forsake any sin I have committed or am about to commit. I have
    to come to the point of total agreement with God's requirements.
- However I must also forgive any person whether they confess, repent or forsake sin,
    for God alone has the right and complete understanding to judge.
- The sanctified life involves three steps -
    To die to self, be willing to suffer for Jesus, be filled with the Holy Spirit.
    The only outward evidence of a spirit-filled life is love, joy and peace.

January 10

WHAT DOES ROMANS 8:28 MEAN ?

For born-again believers, all things work together for good, if they love God and are called to be conformed to the image of Christ. Isolated experiences by themselves can be disappointing or even painful. But when they are handed over to God as an offering with thanksgiving and praise, He puts them together to work out a beautiful end product.
Genesis 50:20; Proverbs 16:7; 1 Corinthians 4:5; Philippians 1:6

Examples from everyday life -

A gorgeous mosaic - Each piece is useless by itself. All have to be handed over to the Lord. If even one piece is missing, the picture will be incomplete.

A delicious cake - It is made up of flour, baking powder, shortening, sugar, raw eggs and flavorings. None of these ingredients can be eaten and enjoyed by themselves. They are like the adversities of life. Only God can blend them together for a gourmet dessert.

A beautiful symphony. The musicians have to play the same score (the Bible), have to be in tune with each other and submit to the leadership of the conductor, Jesus Christ. Then the dissonance of the worldly chaos turns into the harmony of heavenly joy.

CONDITIONS FOR ANSWERED PRAYERS

- We have to confess all sins. They block our access to God. Psalm 66:18
- We have to show reverence and respect to God. Psalm 145:19
- We have to pray in line with God's will. 1 John 5:14-15
- We have to pray in the name of Jesus. John 14:13-14
- We have to forgive others. Mark 11:25
- We have to abide in Christ. John 15:7
- We have to keep God's commandments. 1 John 3:22
- We have to delight in the Lord. Psalm 37:4
- We have to submit and trust in the Lord. Psalm 37:5
- We have to be specific and ask. Matthew 7:7
- We have to ask in faith. James 1:6-8
- We have to give thanks. Philippians 4:6

January 12

REASONS FOR UNANSWERED PRAYERS

- Unconfessed sins. Isaiah 59:2
- More focus on the petitions than God Himself. Psalm 27:4
- Lack of faith. Hebrews 11:6
- Disharmony in the home. 1 Peter 3:7
- Unforgiveness. Matthew 6:14-15
- Wrong motives. James 4:3
- Insensitivity towards others. Proverbs 21:13
- Lack of commitment. Deuteronomy 6:4-9
- A closed Bible. Proverbs 28:9

January 13

WHAT IS FAITH ?
Hebrews 11:1

Faith is the certainty that God is in control.
Faith is the confidence that His promises will be fulfilled.

Faith is believing in advance what only makes sense when looking back.
Faith is the bird that sings in the dark while anticipating the dawn.
Faith is to trust God's goodness, regardless of adverse circumstances.

MAN AS A TRIUNE BEING

SPIRIT   Capacity to comprehend the essential nature of God.
Desire to worship.
Discernment of good and evil.

SOUL   Mind - Instrument for thinking, reasoning, remembering, understanding.
Will - Function for making choices, decisions.
Emotions - Function to feel and act out the data received from the spirit
       and the mind.

BODY   Temple, tabernacle, tent, vehicle.

After the Fall, man had to depend on his own spirit and his own conscience without the security and fellowship of God. Man's soul became the battleground for the spiritual warfare. His body became an unfaithful and unreliable servant.

SPIRITUAL CONSEQUENCES
       Born in sin.
       In bondage to sin.
       Spiritually blind.

PSYCHOLOGICAL CONSEQUENCES
       Mind - Subject to delusions, deceptions, error.
       Will - Subject to weakness, uncertainty.
       Emotions - Subject to guilt, fear, anger, sorrow.

PHYSICAL CONSEQUENCES
       Body - Subject to pain, sickness, aging, death.

       Question : To what extent did Jesus Christ have a fallen nature?

As a human being, He "inherited" from His mother the physical and psychological consequences of man's fallen state. But since He did NOT have a human father, He did NOT "inherit" the spiritual consequences of Adam's sin.

On the cross, He voluntarily took upon Himself the spiritual consequences of EVERY sin and suffered the full penalty thereof, so we might live and be restored to perfect righteousness.

January 15

THE TRANSFORMED LIFE

HOW TO BECOME A CHRISTIAN

- Believe in and accept Jesus Christ as your personal Savior.
    John 3:3; 3:16; 14:6
- Confess and repent. Proverbs 28:13; Acts 17:30; 1 John 1:9-10
- Know the cost of discipleship. Luke 9:23

WHAT TO EXPECT WHEN FILLED WITH THE HOLY SPIRIT

- A thankful heart. Romans 15:13; Ephesians 5:18-20
- Power to witness and bear fruit. John 15:1-17; Acts 1:8
- Jesus Christ will be glorified. John 15:26-27; John 16:13-14

ABIDING IN CHRIST

- Put on the whole armor of God. Ephesians 6:11-18
- Read and study God's Word daily. Psalm 1:2-3; Psalm 119
- Confess and forsake any sin immediately. 1 John 1:9
- Praise the Lord and give thanks for everything. Psalm 100:4; 1 Thessalonians 5:18
- Learn to love the Lord Jesus Christ above everything else. John 14:15,21,23

January 16

THREE VERSIONS OF THE SERENITY PRAYER

"Lord, grant me the peace, joy and contentment to accept the things I cannot change; the guidance, courage and strength to change the things I can, and the wisdom to know the difference."

"Lord, grant me the Fruit of the Spirit (love, joy, peace, patience, gentleness, integrity, meekness, self-control) to accept the things I cannot change; the help of the Holy Spirit (guidance, courage, strength) to change the things I can, and the assurance that all things work together for my good and your glory."

"Lord, fill me with your love, that I may accept the things I cannot change with joy, patience and meekness; that I may change the things I can with gentleness, integrity, faithfulness and self-control; and that I may experience the peace that comes from knowing the difference."

PRAISE AS SEEN IN PSALM 81

COMPONENTS OF PRAISE -

- Acknowledgment of the sovereignty of God. Function of the spirit.
    Job 1:12; Psalm 135:5-6; Isaiah 45:5-6; Daniel 4:35
- Getting to know God and His ways. Function of the mind.
    Romans 12:2; Colossians 3:10; 1 John 4:7-8
- Obedience to God's Word. Function of the will.
    1 Samuel 15:22; Matthew 7:21-23; John 14:15
- Serving with joyfulness of heart. Function of the emotions.
    Deuteronomy 28:47-48; Psalm 100; Psalm 118:24
- Worship. Function of the spirit, soul and body.
    Isaiah 6:1-7; Revelation 4:8-11

REASONS FOR PRAISE -

- God commands it. Praise initiates true worship. Verse 4
- Praise is a witness to the world of God's power and goodness. Verse 5
- Praise expresses our gratitude for salvation. Verse 6
- Praise shows that God answers prayers. Verse 7 a, b
- Praise confirms God's love even when He tests, disciplines and chastens. Verse 7 c

BENEFITS OF PRAISE -

- Purity of worship, that leaves no room for other powers. Verse 9 b
- Personal relationship with God. Verse 10 a
- Manifestation of grace. Verse 10 b
- Enemies are subdued. They can no longer harass us. Verse 14 a
- God will personally deal with our adversaries. Verse 14 b
- Assurance of lasting victories. Verse 15 a
- Provisions for all our needs. Verse 16 a
- Complete satisfaction for the deepest longings of our souls. Verse 16 b

OUR THREE ENEMIES

THE FLESH

> <u>Definition</u> - Our old sinful nature and all the problems that are caused by it.
> <u>Battleground</u> - Body. Romans 7:18-24; Galatians 5:17
> <u>Temptation</u> - Lust of the flesh. Genesis 3:6a; Luke 4:3
> <u>Sins of the body</u> - Impurity, unlawful desires, gluttony, laziness.
> <u>Weapons</u> - The person of Jesus Christ to redeem us from sin. 1 John 1:7
> The Holy Spirit to shield us from sin. Romans 8:5-6; Galatians 5:16
> <u>Examples</u> - Defeat at Ai. Joshua, chapter 7. The reason was unconfessed sin.
> Jesus at the well. He had no sinful nature, but he had a human body with all its frailties and demands. Hebrews 4:15. Being tired. John 4:6. Being thirsty. John 4:7. Being hungry. Matthew 4:2. Being separated from God for taking on our sins. Matthew 27:46
> <u>Deliverance</u> - Confession, repentance, prayer, praise, thanksgiving, worship.

THE WORLD

> <u>Definition</u> - Outer circumstances, sometimes beyond our control.
> <u>Battleground</u> - Soul (mind, will, emotions). Luke 4:5; John 16:33 b
> <u>Temptation</u> - Lust of the eyes. Genesis 3:6 b; Luke 4:6; Matthew 19:21-22
> <u>Sins of the soul</u> - Unbelief, worry, fear, discontentment, greed.
> <u>Weapons</u> - Faith. Matthew 6:33; 1 John 5:4; 2 Chronicles 20:17-22
> <u>Examples</u> - Victory at Jericho. Joshua, chapter 6. Israelites at the Red Sea. Ex 14:10-12
> Storm at sea. Mark 4:37-40
> <u>Deliverance</u> - Confession, repentance, prayer, praise, thanksgiving, worship.

THE DEVIL

> <u>Definition</u> - Deceptions, delusions, error, temptations, accusations.
> <u>Battleground</u> - Spirit. Luke 4:9-11; Ephesians 6:12
> <u>Temptation</u> - Pride of life. Genesis 3:1,4; Job 2:9; Isaiah 14:13-14
> <u>Sins of the Spirit</u> - Pride, idolatry, hatred, malice, unforgiveness, self-centeredness, criticism, dishonesty, temper, rebellion, ingratitude.
> <u>Weapons</u> - Word of God. Psalm 119; Hebrews 4:12; Ephesians 6:17 b
> <u>Examples</u> - Temptation in the Garden of Eden. Genesis 3:1-6. Compromise with the Gibeonites. Joshua, chapter 9. Consequences of unbelief. 2 Thess 2:9-12
> <u>Deliverance</u> - Confession, repentance, prayer, praise, thanksgiving, worship.

DIFFERENT WAYS TO COPE WITH LIFE

RELIGION   says : Hope and pray your way out.

PHILOSOPHY   says : Think your way out.

LEGALISM   says : Obey your way out.

EDUCATION   says : Learn your way out.

MEDICINE   says : Take pills for your way out.

MATERIALISM   says : Spend your way out.

WORLDLINESS   says : Enjoy your way out.

FATALISM   says : Resign your way out.

PSYCHOLOGY   says : Blame others for your way out.

EGOTISM   says : Grab your way out.

INDULGENCE   says : Eat and drink your way out.

HUMANISM   says : Compromise your way out.

SCIENCE   says : Invent your way out.

MILITARISM   says : Fight your way out.

INDUSTRY   says : Work your way out.

LABOR   says : Strike your way out.

DIPLOMACY   says : Talk your way out.

POLITICS   says : Promise your way out.

SOCIALISM   says : Do-good your way out.

COMMUNISM   says : Lie your way out.

LIBERALISM   says : Do as you please for your way out.

Christianity says : Jesus Christ is your only way out.

January 20

A DAILY FITNESS PROGRAM

- Yield every area of your life to the Lordship of Jesus Christ.
    Matthew 7:21-23; John 1:11-12; Romans 10:9
- Confess your sins immediately.
    1 John 1:9
- Accept God's forgiveness and forgive others and yourself.
    Ephesians 4:32
- Spend time alone with God.
    Psalm 27:4; Mark 1:35
- Be continuously filled with the Holy Spirit.
    Acts 13:52; Ephesians 5:18
- Live by the Word of God.
    Psalm 119; Romans 15:4; 2 Timothy 3:16
- Cultivate a renewed mind.
    Romans 12:1-2; 2 Corinthians 10:4-5; Ephesians 4:22-24
- Put on the whole armor of God.
    Ephesians 6:10-18
- Be on the alert constantly.
    James 4:7; 1 Peter 5:8-9
- Practice praise in every situation.
    Psalm 34:1; Psalm 100:4; Ephesians 5:20; Phil 4:4; 1 Thessalonians 5:18
- Maintain a disciplined life.
    Matthew 16:24-25; Romans 12:1
- Cultivate right relationships.
    Matthew 18:15-17; James 4:4; 1 John 2:9-11
- Use your weapons of defense.
    John 14:13; 2 Corinthians 10:3-5; Hebrews 4:12
- Stand up for your convictions.
    Matthew 10:32; Romans 10:9-10

January 21

COUNTING THE COST

THE YOKE - Submission to Christ's way, truth and life. Matthew 11:28-30

THE CROSS - Willingness to die to self in a hostile and sinful world. Matthew 16:24

THE THORN IN THE FLESH - A personal infirmity allowed by God, but made
    bearable through His grace. 2 Corinthians 12:7-10

January 22

PRAYER MOTIVATIONS

- Desire for God to be glorified.

- Desire for fellowship with God.

- Desire to express gratitude for past, present and future blessings.

- Desire for mercy and grace.

- Desire for needs to be met.

- Desire for guidance, discernment and wisdom.

- Desire for deliverance from oppression.

- Desire for salvation for the lost and sanctification for believers.

- Desire for God's will to prevail.

- Desire for the return of the Lord Jesus Christ.

January 23

TODAY I CHOOSE

LOVE - To be a love-giver, not a love-seeker.

JOY - To focus on praise, not problems.

PEACE - To seek harmony, not conflict.

PATIENCE - To affirm that God is in control, not the world, the flesh or the devil.

GENTLENESS - To be kind, not critical.

GOODNESS - To be generous, not selfish.

FAITHFULNESS - To be anchored in the Trinity, not adrift in the world.

MEEKNESS - To compare myself to Jesus, not to others.

SELF-CONTROL - To sacrifice my rights, not dwell on them.

January 24

WHEN THE SPIRIT IS HEAVY AND THERE IS NO JOY

- Realize that you are sitting on the wrong nest and are brooding on the wrong things. To brood means to concentrate on something, to cause it to develop, to give form and substance to, to nurture, to keep alive and make it grow. The kingdom of darkness and the Kingdom of light are like unhatched hen's eggs. We hatch out defeat by brooding on the negative. We hatch out the promises of the Bible by faith and the right attitude of thanksgiving and praise. We have to keep our undivided attention on the sovereignty of God. Joshua 24:15; 1 Kings 18:21; Philippians 4:4

- Recognize the dark forces in the form of heavy burdens Matthew 11:28, unconfessed transgressions Proverbs 28:13 and oppression from the enemy Psalm 43.

- Let the light of Christ shine in the dark places. Put all problems at the foot of the Cross. Picture yourself on a see-saw with Jesus and turn over to Him all adversities, circumstances and people you cannot handle. Praise Him and watch how these very things that have held you down, lift you up as soon as you submit them to Jesus with thanksgiving.

- Lift yourself above the dimension of time and picture yourself in the middle of a great panorama. Behind, you see the crucified Lord redeeming us; above, you see the Lord sitting on the right hand of God interceding for us; before, you see the Lord coming to take us home with Him. From this spiritual vantage point, all problems are solved, all sicknesses healed, all infirmities made whole and all darkness gone.

January 25

PRAYER FOR HIS PRESENCE

The Lord is before me to guide me. Deuteronomy 31:8
The Lord is behind me to protect me. Psalm 139:5
The Lord is beneath me to uphold me. Deuteronomy 33:27
The Lord is all around me to help me. Psalm 46:1
The Lord is near me to comfort me. 2 Corinthians 1:3-4
The Lord is in me to provide love, joy and peace. Galatians 5:22
The Lord is above me to bless me with mercy and grace.
Psalm 23:6; Hebrews 4:16

WHAT IS IMPORTANT ?

HOW TO BE CONNECTED TO THE TRINITY

- To know the will of God and to obey His commandments.
  Psalm 119; Matthew 7:21; John 4:34; 6:38; Romans 12:2
- To have a close relationship with the Lord Jesus Christ.
  Psalm 23; 27:4; 73:25; John 14:23; 1 John 1:3,6; Revelation 3:20
- To be filled with the Holy Spirit.
  Luke 11:13; John 14:16-17; Romans 8:14; 1 Corinthians 3:16; Ephesians 5:18

HOW TO DEAL WITH THE PAST

- To accept that our sins are forgiven and forgotten.
  Psalm 103:12; Isaiah 38:17; Colossians 2:14
- To forgive others.
  Matthew 6:14-15; 18:21-22; Colossians 3:13
- To start anew.
  Romans 6:6-8; 11; Galatians 2:20; Ephesians 4:23-24; Colossians 3:1-3

HOW TO LIVE IN THE PRESENT

- To decide who is Lord.
  Joshua 24:15; Matthew 6:24; John 6:66-68; 2 Corinthians 6:2
- To praise and rejoice in the Lord.
  Psalm 34:1; 113:3; 118:24; Ephesians 5:20; Philippians 4:4; 1 Thessalonians 5:18
- To serve the Lord.
  John 9:4; 12:26; Romans 13:11; Ephesians 5:14-17; Colossians 4:5

HOW TO FACE THE FUTURE

- To trust in the Lord.
  Psalm 37:5; Proverbs 3:3-6; Matthew 6:34
- To have a goal.
  Luke 9:62; Philippians 3:14
- To anticipate the return of the Lord Jesus Christ.
  Titus 2:13; 1 John 2:2

There is no greater joy, satisfaction and comfort than to be in the will of God, abide in Christ and be filled with the Holy Spirit.

DISCERNMENT VERSUS JUDGMENT

DISCERNMENT - "anakrino" means to distinguish.
                   "diakrino" means to investigate.
    It operates in the dispensation of grace to offer solutions to problems.
    It is a spiritual gift. 1 Corinthians 12:10

- Asks questions and shows patience and interest.
- Investigates to discover root causes.
- Finds similar personal problems through introspection.
- Prays for ways to overcome.
- Is submissive to God.
- Accepts the offender.
- Shares solutions from personal experience.
- Assumes responsibility for restoration.
- Extends a helping hand.

JUDGMENT - "krino" means to give a verdict.
        It operates in the dispensation of law without offering solutions.
        It comes from the old nature. Romans 2:1-3

- Accepts hearsay and forms opinions.
- Judges on surface knowledge.
- It is blind to similar personal problems.
- Makes up own solutions.
- The self and the ego are in control.
- Rejects the sin and the sinner.
- Has no personal experience in overcoming.
- Reminds God to step in.
- Points an accusing finger.

January 28

THE PARABLE OF THE SOWER

The Word of God must be received through the regenerated spirit in a person. If it enters through the soul, it will not take roots. Matthew 13: 1-9, 18-23

WAYSIDE - The <u>intellect</u> is incapable of understanding spiritual things. 1 Cor 2:14
THORNY PLACES - The <u>will</u>, through a positive thinking approach, has no stamina.
STONY GROUND - The <u>emotions</u>, through a charismatic approach, are unreliable.
Mind, will and emotions must be in submission to the spirit, not act independently.

January 29

DON'T BE SIDETRACKED

KNOWLEDGE OF THE WORD -

An in-depth Bible study helps us to grow in faith and learn God's way, so we can obey His commandments. Deuteronomy 11:18-20; Psalm 1:2; Psalm 119
Unbalanced and incomplete - Fundamental church. Too much emphasis on intellect, not enough on the heart. 2 Corinthians 3:6; Titus 3:9

PRACTICAL APPLICATION FOR EVERYDAY LIFE -

To put Bible principles into shoe leather. James 1:22; 2:20
Unbalanced and incomplete - Liberal church, all cults and "isms". Emphasis on creed without a biblical foundation. Isaiah 64:6-7; Hosea 4:6; Micah 4:12; Romans 10:1-4

STAYING IN THE MAINSTREAM OF THE HOLY SPIRIT -

To offer thanksgiving, praise and worship to God. Psalm 34:1; Acts 1:8; Romans 8:9
Unbalanced and incomplete - Charismatic church. Tendency to go off on an emotional tangent for lack of biblical knowledge. 1 Corinthians 14:33, 40

January 30

PHONE NUMBERS FROM THE BIBLE

SIN   **316** - John 3:16; **121** - 1 John 2:1; **312** - Jeremiah 3:12

DANGER   **911** - Psalm 91:1; **461** - Psalm 46:1; **571** - Psalm 57:1

ANXIETY   **263** - Isaiah 26:3; **327** - Psalm 32:7; **157** - 1 Peter 5:7

FEAR   **318** - Deuteronomy 31:8; **271** - Psalm 27:1; **536** - Mark 5:36

LONELINESS   **313** - Jeremiah 31:3; **234** - Psalm 23:4; **464** - Isaiah 46:4

ADVICE   **333** - Jeremiah 33:3; **429** - Deuteronomy 4:29; **119** - Luke 11:9

January 31

FOLLOW THE A's TO VICTORY

ADMIT your sins. Proverbs 28:13; 1 John 1:9
ACKNOWLEGE the sovereignty of God. Job 1:21; Daniel 4:35
ABANDON your rights. Matthew 16:24; 26:39
ALONE with God. Matthew 14:23; Mark 1:35
ABIDE in Christ. John 15:4-10; 2 John 9
APPEAL to God's promises. Proverbs 3:5-6; Isaiah 41:10, 13
AFFIRM your faith. Romans 10:9; Hebrews 10:23
ALLOW for God's timing and ways. Isaiah 55:8-9; Matthew 24:44
ATTENTIVE to the Still Small Voice. 1 Kings 19:11-12; Isaiah 30:21
ACT on His directions. James 1:22; 2:20
ALWAYS give thanks and praise. Ephesians 5:20; 1 Thessalonians 5:18

February 1

CHOICE

C ommitment to

      H oliness by

           O vercoming the

                  I through

                        C hrist's

                              E nabling

February 2

HELPFUL HINTS

Anxiety -	HHH	(Hold His Hand)
Depression -	MED	(Medication, Exercise, Dialogue)
Frozen emotions -	LOG	(Lean On Grace)
Frustrations -	TOP	(Trust, Obey, Praise)
Insomnia -	TIM	(Thanksgiving, Intercession, Memorization)
Irritation -	FUR	(Forgiveness, Understanding, Respect)
Oppression -	COD	(Christ Offers Deliverance)
Pride -	IOC	(Imitation Of Christ)
Touchiness -	BTM	(Behold The Man). John 19:5
Regrets -	STP	(Surrender The Past)

February 3

WHAT TO FOCUS ON

Have a goal - To cope in a world of disappointments, problems and pain is to focus on a goal that the <u>World</u> (forces beyond our control), the <u>Flesh</u> (forces of the natural self) and the <u>Devil</u> (forces of evil) cannot derail, sabotage or destroy.

- To produce the 9-fold Fruit of the Spirit as a witness of Christ. Galatians 5:22
- To become an instrument for God's blessings to people, animals, plants and the environment. Isaiah 6:8; Philippians 2:13-15
- To hear God say: "Well done, you good and faithful servant. Come and enter into the joy of the Lord." Matthew 25:21

Have a map - To find and follow the path to that goal.

- Trust in the sovereignty (omniscience, omnipotence, omnipresence) of God. Romans 11:33; Mark 10:27; Psalm 139:5-11
- Obey the holiness of God. Matthew 5:48; Hebrews 10:31; 1 Timothy 6:14-16
- Praise the love of God. Psalm 100; Jeremiah 31:3; John 3:16
- Focus on spiritual values. Matthew 6:19-21; Colossians 3:1-3
- Build on a solid foundation. Matthew 7:24-25; 1 Corinthians 3:11
- Walk by faith. Hebrews 11:6 ; 2 Corinthians 5:7
- Lean on grace. John 1:16-17; 2 Corinthians 12:9-10
- Rest in love. Zephaniah 3:17; Matthew 11:28
- Be in tune with God, in harmony with others and in step with myself.

February 4

WHAT CHRIST IS

THE BREAD - John 6:35
  THE LIGHT - John 8:12
    THE DOOR - John 10:9
      THE GOOD SHEPHERD - John 10:11, 14
        THE RESURRECTION and THE LIFE - John 11:25
          THE WAY, THE TRUTH and THE LIFE - John 14:6
            THE VINE - John 15:5
              THE ALPHA and OMEGA - Revelation 1:8

THE NINE FOLD FRUIT OF THE SPIRIT

LOVE - Total commitment of body, soul and spirit.
John 13:34; 14:15; 1 Corinthians 13:1-8; 1 John 4:7-8

JOY - Happiness, contentment, gladness, delight, gratefulness.
Nehemiah 8:10; Psalm 100; Ephesians 5:20; Philippians 4:4, 11; Thess 5:16, 18

PEACE - Harmony, serenity, tranquility, calmness, security, relaxation, rest.
Isaiah 26:3; John 14:27; 16:33; Eph 2:14; Phil 4:7-9; 1 Thessalonians 5:23

LONG-SUFFERING - Patience, forgiveness, forbearance, endurance, fortitude,
even temper, steadfastness.
Psalm 27:14; Matthew 18:21-22; Ephesians 4:2; Colossians 3:12-14; James 1:2-4

GENTLENESS - Kindness, tenderness, understanding, sensitivity, compassion,
empathy, mercy.
Lamentations 3:22-23; Matthew 11:28-30; Titus 3:2

GOODNESS - Integrity, virtue, moral soundness, benevolence, generosity,
uprightness, honesty.
Psalm 15:2-3; 25:21; 37:3; Proverbs 31:25-30; Ecclesiastes 12:13-14;
1 Timothy 6:11-12; 2 Peter 1:3-7

FAITHFULNESS - Loyalty, sincerity, trustworthiness, consistency, dependability,
accountability, allegiance.
Ruth 1:16-17; Proverbs 18:24; Matthew 25:21; Revelation 2:10

MEEKNESS - Humility, submission, obedience, flexibility, modesty, trust.
Psalm 22:26; Isaiah 57:15; Zephaniah 2:3; Matthew 5:5; Galatians 6:1
Ephesians 4:1-2; 1 Peter 3:4, 15

SELF-CONTROL - Temperance, sobriety, self-restraint, moderation.
Proverbs 16:32; 25:28; Romans 6:11-14; 1 Corinthians 9:27; 1 Peter 2:11

To grow the Fruit

Till the soil by confession, repentance and restitution.
Plant the seed of faith and hope.
Nourish the plant with God's Word.
Water it with prayers.
Shine on it with praise.

February 6

A CONTRACT WITH GOD

<u>MY PLEDGE</u>

To love Him. Luke 10:27

To thank, praise, worship.
        Psalm 29:2; 100:4

To please Him. 2 Corinthians 5:9

To trust Him. Ps 37:5; Proverbs 3:5;
        Isaiah 26:4

To abide in Him. John 15:4

To obey His Word. John 14:23

To pray. Jeremiah 29:12-13; Luke 18:1
        Philippians 4:6; 1 Thess 5:17

To forgive others. Matthew 18:21-22

To be a blessing to others. Matthew 5:44

To run the race. 1 Corinthians 9:24;
        Philippians 3:14; Hebrews 12:1

To be conformed to Christ. Philippians 2:5

To rejoice. Psalm 32:11; 100:1-2;
        Philippians 4:4

<u>GOD's PLEDGE</u>

To love me. Jeremiah 31:3

To be with me. Psalm 22:3

To please me. Luke 12:32; John 10:10

To guide me. Ps 37:8; Proverbs 3:6;
        Isaiah 45:2

To protect me. Psalm 91:1

To keep me well. Deuteronomy 4:40

To respond. 2 Chronicles7:14; Ps 91:15
        Jeremiah 33:3; Philippians 4:7

To forgive me. Matthew 6:14

To bless me. Isaiah 44:3

To reward me. 2 Timothy 4:8;
        Hebrews 11:6; 2 John 8

To conform me to Christ. Romans 8:29

To provide mercy and grace. Ps 23:6;
        Psalm 100:5; Hebrews 4:16

February 7

TO ASK, TO SEEK, TO KNOCK
Matthew 7:7

TO ASK   -   To come to God empty handed like a beggar, but filled with trust like a
        child resting in his father's arms.

TO SEEK -   To add an effort to asking. To seek a job is to do research, send out
        resumes, prepare the mind, groom the appearance, pound the pavement
        and establish a network.

TO KNOCK - To add persistence to the effort and asking. To overcome obstacles,
        set-backs, discouragement and rejection.

NEVER, NEVER, NEVER GIVE UP !!!

February 8

WHATEVER IS NEEDED

Lord, send me whatever I need to be conformed to the image of Jesus Christ.

Happiness or Sorrow
  Health or Sickness
    Freedom or Confinement
      Success or Failure
        Comfort or Pain
          Pleasure or Suffering
            Abundance or Need
              Fullness or Emptiness
                Affirmation or Conviction
                  Reward or Chastisement
                    Tranquility or Turmoil
                      Challenge or Frustration
                        Support or Opposition
                          Fellowship or Solitude
                          Friend or Foe
                            Confidence or Uncertainty
                            Convenience or Hardship

February 9

THE WAY BACK TO WHOLENESS

- Accept and submit to God's plan of redemption. John 3:16; 1 Peter 1:18-19
- Take everything to the cross. Hebrews 7:25; 1 Peter 2:24
- Forgive others and set them free. Matthew 6:14; Colossians 3:13
- Accept forgiveness and restoration. 1 John 1:9; 2.Corinthians 5:17
- Desire intimacy with God. Psalm 27:4; 73:25; Jeremiah 29:13; Philippians 3:9-10
- Make faith and obedience a top priority. Hebrews 11:6; Jeremiah 7:23

The highest motive for obeying God comes from a grateful heart that wants to please
HIM.

LORD, deliver me from an immature fear of punishment by developing in me a deep
awareness of your love and a profound desire to please you.

February 10

TO BE AN INTERCESSOR

Prayer is not something we <u>do</u> - it is something we <u>are</u>. It is not a certain time set apart going over a prayer list, but a 24 hour abiding in Christ as a way of life. To pray for others is to stand in the gap and build a bridge. Identify with the interest and desire God has for them. Ezekiel 22:30; Romans 1:9; Colossians 1:9-11; 1 Timothy 2:1-4

An intercessor has to -

- Be purified, sanctified and called. Psalm 24:3-4; Malachi 3:3; 1 Peter 2:9
- Accept others as they are and respect their free will and choices. Abstain from Irritation, frustration, projection, manipulation, arm-twisting, criticism, contempt and condemnation. Matthew 7:1-5; Romans 14:13; 1 Corinthians 4:5
- Be a vessel, transmitter and instrument for God to bring His light into the confusion of their lives. Daniel 12:3; Matthew 5:14-16; Ephesians 5:8; Philippians 2:14-16
- To offer encouragement, guidance, help, healing and hope. Romans 12:13-18; 1 Thessalonians 2:11; 5:14
- Focus on God's ultimate goal for them, which is the conformation to Christ. Romans 8:29-30; 1 Corinthians 15:49
- Look forward to spending eternity with them in the glorious presence of Love, Joy and Peace personified. John 14:1-3; 1 Corinthians 2:9
- Leave the entire process in the hands of God. Philippians 1:6; 2 Timothy 1:12

February 11

THREE TYPES OF CLOTHING

INNOCENCE - When we were created, our body and our true, unique personality were wrapped in innocence. Nothing had to be hidden.

FIG LEAVES - Innocence was lost by sin, and we became naked, vulnerable and contaminated. Our true self was pushed into the subconscious, and we tried to cover up our shame and guilt by hiding our depravity.

ROBE OF RIGHTEOUSNESS - Through Christ we can become new creations and receive a new identity He purchased for us by His blood at Calgary. The complete transformation will be manifested and made visible when Christ returns to take us home to heaven.

February 12

PARADISE LOST

There is a pervasive and chronic pain in my life as I stand in front of the Garden of Eden, rattling the gate, realizing that I have no way to go back in.

Why am I so sad?

- Because of my damaged soul and aging body.
- Because of being disconnected from people and the mainstream of life.
- Because of the overwhelming evil in the world.
- Because of the deterioration of the environment.
- Because I don't feel God's presence as a tangible reality.

A rocky road ahead.

- My deepest longings can never be satisfied in this life. The things I can enjoy now are no more than appetizers. The real feast is yet to come.
- All I can do now is to develop a taste of intimacy with Christ that I feel only sporadically now in this life.
- Until I attain unity with Christ in heaven, the inconsolable longing for more will remain in my heart.
- Suffering is inevitable, but the hope for the future is more valuable than a temporary relief.
- When all my prayers and efforts fail to ease the problems, I become desperate enough to seek God for His fellowship and not only for His solutions.
- A sense of an impending union with Someone I have never met, but have always known, make me come alive with great anticipation.
- Then the excitement fades, and I find myself still outside of Paradise.
- I must keep my focus on the eternity ahead while trying to live in harmony with God.
- The choices I make today determine the quality of what has passed and the rewards that lay in the future.

February 13

TWO KEYS FOR OPENING PARADISE

THE DESIRE OF MY HEART - It is not relief from pain, but to find God.
Jeremiah 29:13

THE WILL OF GOD - It is not to spare me from pain, but to draw me to Him.
Jeremiah 31:3

THE EPISTLE OF JAMES

THE PERSON - James, the half-brother of Jesus, but he calls himself
a servant of God and the Lord Jesus Christ. James 1:1

THE PURPOSE - Guidelines for Christian living. The proof of our faith
is a transformed life. James 2:26

THE PROMISE - Reward for persevering in trials and suffering afflictions.
James 1:12; 5:7-11

Did you know that you are precious in God's sight?
He loves you so much that He wants to spend eternity with you.

February 15

LOVE AND ETERNITY
Galatians 5:22-23

JOY is love's exuberance.
PEACE is love's rest.
PATIENCE is love's endurance.
GENTLENESS is love's expression.
INTEGRITY is love's standard.
FAITHFULNESS is love's trademark.
MEEKNESS is love's unselfishness.
SELF-CONTROL is love's discipline.

Psalm 145:13

What is *ETERNITY* ?

It is timeless existence. Suppose God sent a dove to earth every thousand years to pick up one grain of sand and bring it back to heaven. When all the beaches, ocean floors and riverbeds had been carried away, eternity would have only begun.

February 16

A WITNESS TO CHRIST

The best way to be a Christian witness is when others see in us The Fruit of the Spirit.

LOVE - A B C of love.
JOY - 1 Chronicles 16:10 "Glorify God by seeking Him with a joyful heart."
       Psalm 107:22 "Offer the sacrifice of thanksgiving and declare His works with rejoicing."
PEACE - Isaiah 26:3 "You can have perfect peace when you keep your eyes on Him."
       John 16:33 "You can have peace in the midst of turmoil, because I have overcome the world."
       Phil 4:6-7 "Worry about nothing; pray about everything; rejoice always."
LONG-SUFFERING - James 5:10 "Remember the prophets as examples of patiently enduring afflictions."
GENTLENESS - Matthew 11:29 "I am gentle and humble at heart."
INTEGRITY - 2 Corinthians 3:2 "Others watch our behavior."
FAITHFULNESS - Luke 16:10 "To be totally honest."
MEEKNESS - 1 Peter 3:4 "The inner beauty is a meek and quiet spirit."
SELF-CONTROL - 1 Corinthians 8:9 "Don't be a stumbling block to others."
       1 Corinthians 10:32 "Give no offense to others."

February 17

AN INSTRUMENT OF GOD

What I can do right now, regardless of outer or inner circumstances.

• To be in tune with God - Keep your eyes on Jesus.
• To be in harmony with God - Give thanks and praise for everything.
• To be in step with God - Do the task at hand.

I WILL –

Thank (appreciate)
Honor (respect, esteem)
Praise (declare worthy)
Magnify (focus, declare important)
Exalt (lift on high, proclaim)
Glorify (worship)

THE LORD AT ALL TIMES -

February 18

COMPONENTS OF MUSIC

TO BE IN TUNE WITH GOD

- To acknowledge sins by comparing out of tune attitudes to God's perfect pitch.
- To repent by correcting and adjusting the mind.
- To obey by playing under God's directions.

TO BE IN HARMONY WITH OTHERS

- To agree on the key signature and script.
- To interact in a relationship involves creating a melody and accompaniment.
- To mix major keys (joy, happiness) with minor keys (sorrow, compassion).
  Sharps are stimulating, Flats are calming.
- To add vitality to a relationship with occasional dissonance, that will resolve.

TO BE IN STEP WITH MYSELF

- To accept the personality that God created in me.
- To adjust my heartbeat, pulse, rhythm, cadence and pace to a way of life that
  brings glory to God.

February 19

SELF IN CONTROL

When self is on the throne, Satan has legal access to the spirit, soul and body.
PRIDE - Self enters the spirit realm to raise self-esteem, control and power and
        to drown out the guilt so there is no need for Christ's atonement.
        Self-sufficiency is rebellion against God's plan for mankind.
        Gen 3:1-6; 1 Sam 15:23; Psalm 10:4; Prov 16:18; Isa 14:13-14

Having replaced God as top authority, a vacuum is created in the heart of man.
IDOLATRY - Man tries to fill this void with money, religion, work, people,
        spouses, children, things, prestige, food, alcohol, drugs and sex.
        Ex 20:3-6; Isa 42:8; Jer 2:13; 1 Cor 10:14; 1 John 5:21

When all these "gods" fail to satisfy, there is anger, violence and despair.
BITTERNESS - Man blames God, others, the world and refuses to repent.
        Deut 28:47-48; Matt 18:32-35; Rom 1:21-22; Hebr 12:14-15

TEN REASONS WHY WE SUFFER

- We suffer when there are unconfessed sins in our lives. Psalm 38:3-8
  Our conscience makes us uncomfortable in order to seek forgiveness at the cross.
  Acts 9:8-9

- We suffer when we are chastened by the Lord. 2 Sam 12:10-14; Psalm 32:3-4;
  Hebrews 12:6. Our hearts need to be purified. Isaiah 1:25

- We suffer for our past sins. Jeremiah 12:13. We live in an orderly universe that
  operates by fixed laws of cause and effect. Galatians 6:7-8

- We suffer for our thoughtless, foolish mistakes. 1 Peter 2:20. Some lessons are
  learned only the hard way. Proverbs 22:15

- We suffer because of the conflict between our old Adamic nature and our new
  status in Christ. Romans 7:15-24. There is a power struggle for control in our lives
  between the Holy Spirit and our own self. Romans 8:7-8

- We suffer both physically and emotionally because of God's curse on His
  creation. Genesis 3:14-19. The vulnerability and the aging of our bodies, the hazards
  and dangers are all around us. Romans 8:22-23

- We suffer because of other people's sins. Numbers 14:33-34
  The dispositions, decisions, actions and mistakes of other people have a profound
  influence on our lives, because we all depend on each other. 1 John 3:15-17

- We suffer because we are in the midst of a spiritual warfare. Daniel 10:13
  Satan and his angels are still on the loose. 1 Peter 5:8. They have to get permission from God to
  touch true Christians. Job 1:12

- We suffer persecution when openly taking a stand for the Truth. 2 Timothy 3:12
  The Gospel provokes the hatred of Satan and the guilt of sinners. John 15:18

- We suffer when God tests our faith. 2 Corinthians 4:8-11. God allows adversities to
  build up our own spiritual fitness and become witnesses for Him to the world and Satan, and an
  inspiration to other Christians. Acts 7:54-60

God allows adversity for a specific purpose.
> God may or may not reveal the reason.
>> Adversity can be a gift from God.
>>> Satan can be a messenger or agent.
>>>> Adversity is meant to help, not hinder spiritual growth.
>>>> God will comfort us in the midst of adversities.

February 21

PARAPHRASE OF HABAKKUK 3:17-19

THOUGH THE FIG TREE DOES NOT BLOSSOM -
> There is nothing to look forward to in the future.

THERE IS NO FRUIT ON THE VINE -
> There is no joy in my life.

THOUGH THE OLIVE TREE FAILS -
> There is nothing to soothe my wounds.

AND THE FIELDS PRODUCE NO CROP -
> I am barren, unproductive and useless.

THOUGH THE FLOCKS ARE CUT OFF FROM THE FOLD -
> I am disconnected, abandoned and lonely.

AND THERE ARE NO CATTLE IN THE BARN -
> I am vulnerable, insecure and worried.

NEVERTHELESS I WILL FOCUS ON THE GOODNESS OF THE LORD -
> I will seek God for who He is, and not merely for the satisfaction He provides.

AND REJOICE IN HIM AS MY LORD AND SAVIOR -
> I will be grateful for what He has done to redeem me.

HE WILL GIVE ME STRENGTH IN THE MOUNTAINS, COMFORT IN THE VALLEYS,
> *PROVISIONS IN THE DESERT, COURAGE IN DANGER,*
> *PEACE IN TURMOIL, GUIDANCE IN THE FOG and LIGHT IN DARKNESS -*
> He enables me to gain a new understanding of Him and a new perspective of what is going on in the world.

February 22

WHAT IS JOY ?

- Joy is an inward song that cannot be silenced by adverse circumstances.
- Joy is a gift of God that we receive with thanksgiving.
- Joy cannot be produced by one's own efforts.
- Joy is a byproduct of a growing relationship between God and us.
- Joy must have its' roots in the Godhead.
- Joy can be found in the presence of God, in our walk with Jesus and in our obedience to the Holy Spirit.

February 23

A FORK IN THE ROAD
Jeremiah 6:16

The way to light -

- *OBEDIENCE TO GOD* - The desire to connect with God and come to Him on His terms.

The way to darkness -

- *INDEPENDENCE* - The desire to preserve individual rights and way of life.

- *NEW AGE* - An attempt to reach God without Christ.

- *ASTROLOGY* - Consultation of the dark forces.

- *HUMANISM* - A non-theistic movement that teaches that man is capable of ethical conduct and self-fulfillment without recourse to a higher, supernatural power.

- *OCCULTISM* - Slavery to the rulers of darkness.

February 24

A DESIRE TO PRAY

Prayer and intercession are not primarily an attempt to reach God with our pleas, but the willingness to let God transmit His power through us.

- *MAKE PRAYER YOUR LIFE* - Giving thanks, stating the needs, voicing feelings, pleading urgently, waiting patiently, persevering steadfastly, interceding faithfully.

- *MAKE YOUR LIFE A PRAYER* - Maintaining an emotional balance by seeking the will of God and accepting help from Christian counselors, Twelve Step groups and medication, if necessary.

Eph 6:18 "Pray on every occasion, as the Spirit leads. Keep alert and never give up."

Romans 12:1 "I want to offer my spirit, soul and body to God as a living sacrifice to serve, glorify and worship Him."

February 25

THE PROGRESSION OF SANCTIFICATION

TO GET TO KNOW CHRIST -
- Casual acquaintance with Jesus.
- Occasional visits.
- Becoming friends.
- Faithful companions.
- Being inseparable.
- Fusion into oneness.

ONENESS WITH CHRIST RESULTS IN -

- Being a witness. Matthew 5:14-16; Acts 1:8; 1 Peter 3:15
- Being an intercessor. Psalm 106:23; Dan 9:16-19; Rom 1:9; Col 1:9-11; 1 Tim 2:1-4
- Being secure in God's love. Jer 31:3; John 10:27-29; Rom 8:35-39; 1 John 3:1-2

February 26

TWO KINDS OF GRIEF

BITTER GRIEF is like an infected wound that festers and doesn't heal. Imbedded in it
are resentment, anger, self-pity and despair.

GENTLE GRIEF is cushioned by an supernatural sweetness when the wound is bathed
in praise, and the situation is released to the healing love of God.
Example : Return a loved-one to the Creator as an expression of
gratitude, faith and hope.

Sorrow is part of life, but it is only temporary.
Psalm 30:5; Isaiah 53:3; 61:3; Joel 2:25; John 16:33; Romans 8:18

Remember   ----------   Never blame, complain or compare.

There is incredible power in the vibes we send out, affecting others with negative forces like spiritual blockages, mental paralysis and physical ailments. Or we can intercede by asking God to set the captives free in spirit, soul and body.

February 27

WHAT HAPPENS AT SALVATION ?

- We are called. 1 Thessalonians 5:24
- We are reconciled to God. 2 Corinthians 5:18
- We are redeemed. Romans 3:24
- All condemnation is removed. Romans 8:1
- All trespasses are forgiven. Psalm 103:2
- We are under grace. Ephesians 2:8
- We are justified. Romans 4:25
- We are dead to the old life. Romans 6:8
- We are free from the law. Romans 8:2
- We are regenerated. Titus 3:5
- We are adopted. Romans 8:15

February 28

- We are accepted by God. Ephesians 1:6
- We are declared righteous. Philippians 3:9
- We are registered in heaven. Luke 10:20
- We are delivered from Satan. Colossians 1:13
- We are transferred into God's kingdom. Colossians 1:13
- We are placed on a sure foundation. Psalm 40:2
- We are appointed priests of God. 1 Peter 2:9
- We are chosen for service. Titus 2:14
- We have access to God. Romans 5:2
- We are under God's care. Philippians 4:19

February 29

- We inherit all His riches. Ephesians 1:18
- We are heirs of God and joint heirs of Christ. Romans 8:17
- We are partners with Christ. 1 Corinthians 1:9
- We receive eternal life. John 3:16
- We are members of the family of God. Ephesians 2:19
- We receive the Holy Spirit. Romans 5:5
- We are complete in Him. Colossians 2:10
- We possess every spiritual blessing. Ephesians 1:3
- We have spiritual perception. 1 Corinthians 2:12
- All scar tissue has been removed from our soul. Isaiah 43:25
- We will be glorified. Romans 8:30

March 1

TO BE EMOTIONALLY WHOLE

INTIMACY WITH GOD -
>To cleanse, warm and recharge myself by the fire of God's love.
>Jeremiah 29:13; 31:3; Hebrews 4:16; Revelation 3:20

INTEGRITY FOR MYSELF -
>Commitment to holiness. Leviticus 20:7; Psalm 41:12; 2 Corinthians 7:1

INTERCESSION FOR OTHERS -
>To share and transmit God's love, joy and peace with others.
>Psalm 106:23; Colossians 1:9-11; 1 Timothy 2:1-4

INVOLVEMENT IN LIFE -
>To release the frozen feelings, to share and witness, to explore and be active.
>Psalm 33:3; 40:3; 150; Isaiah 42:10-12; John 8:36; 2 Timothy 1:6-7

March 2

HEALTH FOR BODY, SOUL AND SPIRIT

BODY - Romans 14:8; 1 Corinthians 6:19-20; Galatians 2:20
>*CPR* - Confess : 2 Chronicles 7:14; Proverbs 28:13; 1 John 1:9
>Purge : Romans 13:12-14; 2 Corinthians 7:1; Hebrews 12:1
>Return : Isaiah 55:7; Luke 15:18; James 4:7-10

Remember : "Nothing tastes as good as cleanliness feels."
>Proverbs 23:1-3; Daniel 1:8; 1 Corinthians 10:13

SOUL - Deuteronomy 31:6; Jeremiah 31:3; 2 Corinthians 12:9
>*TOP* - Trust : Psalm 62:8; 34:8; Proverbs 3:5
>Obey : Joshua 22:5; Luke 6:46; John 14:15
>Praise: Psalm 92:1-2; 100; 103:1-2

Remember: "You can trust, obey and praise anywhere, anytime."
>Psalm 112:7; 119:44; 34:1

SPIRIT - 2 Chronicles 20:15; 2 Corinthians 10:4; 1 John 4:4
>*WAR* - Word : Matthew 4:4-10; Ephesians 6:17; Hebrews 4:12
>Abide : Psalm 91:1; Matthew 11:28-30; John 15:4
>Resist : Ephesians 6:13; James 4:7; 1 Peter 5:8-9

Remember: "You can always stay in the Word, abide in Christ and flee temptation."
>Psalm 119:50; 1 John 2:6; Psalm 119:11

March 3

LOVE AND RESPECT

Why does God tell a husband to love his wife (Ephesians 5:25),
> and a wife to respect her husband (Ephesians 5:33) ?

Masculinity - The cognitive function is in the <u>head</u>. There lies the ability to
> initiate, organize, analyze, edit, define, construct and lead.

Femininity -   The intuitive function is in the <u>heart</u>. There lies the ability to
> respond, receive, nurture, sense, perceive, feel and follow.

<u>Respect</u> is the assurance to the husband, that his authority will be accepted.
<u>Love</u> is the assurance to the wife, that the power of authority will not be abused.

March 4

UNHEALTHY RELATIONSHIPS

- CODEPENDENCY - A desperate and futile attempt to connect with others
> for the purpose of seeking approval and self-esteem,
> relief from guilt and expecting fulfillment for personal needs.
- CONTROL - To have a grip on others and boss them around.
- IRRITATION - To become infected and contaminated by the behavior of others.
- WORRY - To cast a dark spell on others.
- UNFORGIVENESS - To make a fist in the jar of hate.

March 5

A PERSONAL GARDEN

My heart is a garden named "Eden". It has the potential to be a blessing or a curse. I can choose what to sow and how to maintain it. The result will be either flowers, weeds or a desert. Thistles and thorns can choke the flowers, my joy of life. I am what I think in my heart. (Proverbs 23:7; Matthew 12:35) My thoughts, ideas, convictions and words are the seeds, and I can choose which ones to plant. The harvest will be beautiful or ugly, abundant or scarce. I am solely responsible for my garden.
Events and circumstances are not life-bearing seeds - my response to them are.
Today I am planting a new garden. I will follow God's instruction in Psalm 119.

March 6

FROM PALM SUNDAY TO EASTER

- *PALM SUNDAY.* Matthew 21:9
  Triumphant entry into Jerusalem. The first step to a victorious breakthrough is thanksgiving, praise and adoration. Ps 34:1; Ephesians 5:20; 1 Thessalonians 5:18

- *FOOT WASHING.* John 13:4-17
  Cleansing by confession and repentance. Luke 13:3; 1 John 1:8-10
  In humility. James 4:6,10; Through love. John 13:34-35; 1 John 4:7-8
  By forgiveness. Matthew 6:14-15; 18:21-22; In service. Matt 7:12; Galatians 6:2

- *THE LAST SUPPER.* Matthew 26:26-28
  To become one with the Lord Jesus Christ by partaking of Him as the Bread of Life
  in Communion. John 6:48-51; as the Word of Life in Scripture. 1 John 1:1
  Spend time in fellowship with Jesus.

- *THE GARDEN OF GETHSEMANE.* Matthew 26:36-44
  Prayer of preparation to draw strength and guidance for ourselves, 1 Thess 5:17
  Intercession for others. Matthew 5:44; Luke 22:31-32.
  Total submission to the will of God. John 5:30

- *CARRYING THE CROSS.* Matthew 27:29-32
  Counting the cost of discipleship. Luke 9:23
  Willingness to suffer for Christ's sake. Philippians 1:29; 1 Peter 2:20-21

- *CRUCIFICTION.* Matthew 27:50
  Dying to ourselves. Romans 6:3-13; 2 Corinthians 4:10-12
  We have no rights, only privileges. Galatians 5:13; Matthew 23:10; Mark 14:36

- *BURIED IN THE TOMB.* Matthew 27:59-60
  Time of exercising our faith, waiting patiently. Mark 5:35-36; Hebrews 11:1, 6
  Being steadfast overcomers against all odds.
  Revelation 2:7, 17, 26; 3:5, 12, 21; 21:7

- *EASTER.* Matthew 28:1-10
  The ultimate victory.
  "I am the Resurrection and the Life." John 11:25
  "Be of good cheer, I have overcome the world." John 16:33

SOURCES OF ANGER

Causes of anger from the inside - *OUR OWN SINS*

- PRIDE, CONTROL. To be in the driver's seat deciding what to do, how to do it
          and when to do it concerning other people.
      Remedy - To delegate and release. 2 Chronicles 20:12, 15, 17
          To humble ourselves. James 4:6; 1 Peter 5:5-6
- FEAR, WORRY. Failure to see the overall picture. Faith is replaced by doubt.
      Remedy - Put on the "glasses" of faith. 2 Kings 6:16-17; Hebrews 11:1
- SELF-PITY, INGRATITUDE. To focus on the negative.
      Remedy - Give thanks for the situation just as it is. Psalm 34:1-4

Causes of anger from the outside - *SINS OF OTHERS*

- CRITICISM. Examine whether it is justified.
      Remedy - Ask for God's help. Psalm 139:23-24
          Pray for the accusers. Matthew 5:44
- PHYSICAL and EMOTIONAL PAIN. Seek medical help. Adjust attitude.
      Remedy - Incorporate your pain with the suffering of Christ.
          Hebrews 12:2-4; 1 Peter 4:12-13, 19
- POLITICAL INJUSTICE. Discern when to express righteous anger.
      Remedy - Express it in a legitimate way.
          Romans 12:17-21; Ephesians 4:26-27

March 8

RELEASE FROM ANGER

- Remember God's grace and forgiveness to you.
- Repent of your attitude of bitterness.
- Recognize the other person as a tool in God's hand.
- Release the other person from your grip.
- Rely on God's help through friends, books, tapes, therapy and prayer.
- Rejoice and give thanks for the whole experience.

March 9

HIS WORD ---- OUR PRAISE

TWO LEGS TO STAND ON - Obedience and Trust

TWO ARMS TO HUG - Truth and Love

TWO WINGS TO FLY - Faith and Hope

W W W - Work and Walk the Word.
- Focus on God's purpose. Romans 8:29
- Focus on God's method. Isaiah 53:6
- Focus on God's instruction. Psalm 119

These are the tools, equipment, gear, compass and light for getting out of the swamp, finding our way through the woods, enjoying the meadow, crossing the river, climbing the mountain, descending to the valley, trekking through the desert, battling heat, cold, rain, drought, storms, fog, darkness and adversities from within and without.

P P P - Persevere in Practicing Praise.
- Focus on God's sovereignty. Isaiah 40:10-31
- Focus on God's holiness. Psalm 99:9
- Focus on God's love. Jeremiah 31:3

The ladder of faith can only be climbed by faith. The power of God is released when we stand firm in our faith that God is in perfect and loving control of every detail in our life.
We express that faith by praising and thanking Him for any situation we are in. Faith does not originate in our emotions, our feelings or our senses. Faith is a matter of the will. We decide to perceive as real facts what is not revealed to our senses. It is in God Himself, based on His Word.

March 10

A TURN-AROUND
1 Peter 3:9

We can neutralize the acid from the enemy by applying biblical principles and turn a downfall into an uplift.

- Indifference - Compassion - Love. Zechariah 7:9; 1 John 4:7
- Sorrow - Praise - Joy. Psalm 113:3; Psalm 30:5
- Anxiety - Trust - Peace. Joshua 1:9; Isaiah 26:3
- Frustration - Pause - Patience. Psalm 130;5-6; Habakkuk 2:3
- Irritation - Focus on Jesus - Gentleness. Titus 3:2; 1 Peter 2:23
- Weariness - Persistence - Faithfulness. 1 Corinthians 15:58; Galatians 6:9
- Dishonesty - God's omniscience - Integrity. Hebrews 4:13; Matthew 5:48
- Pride - Submission - Meekness. James 4:6-7; 1 Peter 3:4

March 11

IN TIMES OF DROUGHT

Here is a survival kit when spiritual energy runs low.

- Hand over your circumstances to the Lord.
- Trust Him without anxiety.
- Obey His will as you know it.
- Start sharing the Truth that you do have, and He will multiply it.

LOVE - Practice the ABC of love. Romans 5:5; 1 John 4:19
JOY - Give thanks. Play music. Ephesians 5:20; Phil 4:4; 1 Thessalonians 5:18
PEACE - Trust God. Relax and breathe deeply. Ps 119:165; Isaiah 26:3; 1 Peter 3:11
PATIENCE - Understand God's perspective. Romans 8:25; 2 Peter 3:8
GENTLENESS - Respond with kindness. Matthew 11:29; Ephesians 4:2
INTEGRITY - God and people are watching. 2 Corinthians 3:2; Hebrews 12:1
FAITHFULNESS - Be consistent in small things. Matthew 25:21; 1 Timothy 1:12
MEEKNESS - Take the back seat. 2 Corinthians 3:5; 1 Peter 3:4
SELF-CONTROL - Take care of your body. Psalm 39:1; 1 Corinthians 6:19-20

March 12

LIFE WITHOUT GOD

INIQUITY   -   It originates in the Spirit and contaminates the mind and body.
            Isaiah 14:12-14; Ezekiel 28:15
        Result - Separation from God. Isaiah 59:2; Matthew 13: 41-42
        Remedy - To be born again. John 3:16; 14:6; Hebrews 10:19-22

SIN - Rejection of grace, self-effort, works of the flesh. Isa 64:6; Dan 5:27; Rom 3:23
        Result - Guilt, distorted self-image. Romans 7:18-19; 1 Cointhians 3:12-13
        Remedy - Confess, repent, submit. 2 Corinthians 5:21; 1 John 1:9

TRANSGRESSION - Willful disobedience, breaking the law. Jer 2:19; Hebr 6:4-6
        Result - Death. Ezekiel 18:20-24; Romans 6:23
        Remedy - Confess, repent, submit. Psalm 32:5; Proverbs 28:13

Every time we take a step away from God, we yield ground to Satan.
        He will build a stronghold on the ground that was surrendered to him.
                What we will be tomorrow depends on the choices we make today.
                If we make excuses for our sins, they will not be excused.

March 13

BAD CHOICES

When our focus shifts away from God -

- We begin to listen to the wrong voices.
- We will be easily deceived.
- We become proud and insist on our personal rights.
- We make decisions that appeal to the flesh.
- We make excuses for our actions.
- Other people will be hurt.
- We miss out on God's best.

Questions to ask when facing temptations -

- Am I violating Scripture if I indulge in this activity?
- What are the consequences I might have to face?
- What happened to other people who made wrong choices?
- How will this sin affect me?
- Am I willing to pay the price?
- Will it satisfy me or stir up stronger desires?

Since the Holy Spirit lives in me, Christ never leaves me and God knows and sees everything I do, it is impossible to sin in isolation.

March 14

GOING DOWN

FIRST STEP - Doubting God's goodness. Genesis 3:1-5. Shifting the focus from God to self.

SECOND STEP - Disobeying God's commandments. Genesis 3:6 Since God is not reliable to meet my needs, I will provide my own happiness.

THIRD STEP - Pride. Isaiah 14:13-14 I am in charge.

FOURTH STEP - Ingratitude. Romans 1:21-22 I take all the credit and glory for my success and blame God for failures and adversities.

Holiness is not contagious, but sin is. In order to live in an imperfect, corrupt and sinful world, we must either live in isolation or by God's Word. We cannot control our circumstances, but we can choose our attitudes.

Prayer is not conquering God's reluctance, but taking hold of His willingness.

March 15

WHAT TO EXPECT

Life is an ongoing learning process for the purpose of sanctification to transform us into the image of Christ. God will do whatever it takes to make us holy.
Knowing that God is good and His love unconditional, dissolves the fear of taking risks.
Nothing can touch us that is not meant for our ultimate good. Life is not perfect, there will be pain, sorrow, injustice and frustrations, but by keeping up the intimacy with Jesus,
trust in God and obedience to the Holy Spirit, we will be in God's will, which is the safest place to be.
When confronting any situation or circumstance, see all events as learning opportunities.
Don't let minor irritations or major frustrations fool you into thinking that life would be more tolerable without them. They are part of the sanctifying curriculum and all that matters is how we cope with them. We always have a choice either to react or respond.

March 16

COMMITMENT TO THE TRINITY

- *JESUS CHRIST* - Intimacy. To seek, pursue, establish and maintain a personal
  relationship with the Shepherd.
  Psalm 23; Matthew 11:28-30; John 10:14

- *GOD* - Trust. To decide to see God's goodness regardless of the circumstances.
  Even though there is fog - the mountain tops are clear.
  Even though the night is dark - the sun is still in orbit.
  Even though it is Good Friday - Easter is coming.
  Genesis 50:20; Psalm 34:8; Jeremiah 29:11; 31:3

- *HOLY SPIRIT* - Obedience. To persevere in an attitude of submission,
  teachability, dedication and praise.
  Psalm 119:30,35; Jeremiah 7:23; Luke 6:46; John 14:23

Our physical life on this earth begins with birth (starting gate) and death (exit point).
Our spiritual life on this earth begins with death to self by the Cross of Christ and ends in
the transformation of the soul by the return of Christ.

We enter this sanctification process by FAITH. Hab 2:4; Rom 5:1, 10:9; Hebr 11:1
We keep going by HOPE. Ps 16:8; Ps 119:147; Lam 3:24-26; Rom 5:2,5; 1 John 3:2-3
We learn to LOVE. John 13:34; Romans 12:9-12; 1 Corinthians 13; 1 John 4:21

March 17

FAITH - HOPE - LOVE
1 Corinthians 13:13

The path from Faith to Love is Hope. Just as God has given everybody a certain measure of faith, He has also given each living soul an infinite yearning for love. By faith, we can see love beckoning in the distance. The hope to reach that love creates energy to climb every mountain, cross every stream, trek through arid deserts, fend off enemies, counteract discouragement and keep us going.

When the journey is finally over, and we see our object of love, the Lord Jesus Christ, face to face, the road map of faith and hope has accomplished it's mission.

FAITH will be rewarded. Hebrews 11:6
HOPE will be fulfilled. Titus 2:13
LOVE continues into eternity. 1 John 4:16

March 18

ASCENDING PRAYERS

- If I pray for my own needs, God will sustain me through each day.
- If I pray for the needs of my family, God will bring each member into a closer walk with Him.
- If I pray for the needs of the world, God will prepare it for the Second Coming of Christ.
- If I offer thanksgiving, praise and worship, I break through the ceiling of limitation
    Into the realm of the Spirit and the Truth.
    John 4:24; 2 Corinthians 3:16-17

March 19

WALKING WITH GOD

The importance is not <u>where</u> we walk, but with <u>whom</u> we walk.

- Walking by faith is a decision of the mind.
- Walking fearlessly - God is in charge of any situation. Justice will prevail.
- Walking faithfully is a commitment to obedience.
- Walking fruitfully is bringing glory to God.

SURVIVING THE STORMS OF LIFE
Acts 27:1-44; 28:1

- Get rid of cumbersome cargo. Acts 27:18-19
    Pain from the past. Fear of the future.

- Focus on what really matters. Acts 27:22-24
    Today's assignment.

- Let go of the lifeboats. Let go of the anchors. Acts 27:30-32, 40
    Family, friends, counselors, roots, acceptance, connections.

- Get back to a healthy routine. Acts 27:33-34
    Spirit - Focus, prayer, praise.
    Soul - Scripture, attitude, goal.
    Will - Choice, obedience, discipline.
    Emotions - Impression, expression, dialogue.
    Body - Diet, exercise, relaxation.

There is perfect calm in the "eye of the storm". God has said it. And so it is!
Psalm 46:1-11; Isaiah 43:1-3; Matthew 8:23-27

March 21

THE LORD'S PRAYER
Matthew 6:9-13

GOD'S PATERNITY - Our Father.
　　GOD'S PERSON - Fear His holiness.
　　　　GOD'S PROGRAM - Trust His sovereignty.
　　　　　　GOD'S PURPOSE - Submit to His will.
　　　　　　　　GOD'S PROVISION - Grace is sufficient.
　　　　　　　　　　GOD'S PARDON - Receive and grant forgiveness.
　　　　　　　　　　　　GOD'S PREEMINANCE - Worship.

March 22

GOD'S PURPOSE FOR TRIALS

- CLEANSING - Bad attitudes will surface under stress.
    Proverbs 25:4; Isaiah 1:25; 2 Timothy 2;21

- COMPANIONSHIP - God's reason for creating us is to have an intimate
    relationship with us.
    Jeremiah 31:3; Matthew 23:37; John 14:23

- CONVICTION - Trouble offers us a choice of belief systems.
    Joshua 24:15; 1 Kings 18:21; John 6:66-69

- CONFORMITY - Once we choose God's way, He will conform us to the
    image of Christ.
    Romans 8:29; 1 Corinthians 15:49; 2 Corinthians 3:18

- COMPASSION - Suffering will enable us to comfort others.
    2 Corinthians 1:4; 2:7-8; 1 Thessalonians 5:14

March 23

GOD'S PROMISES DURING TRIALS

ASSURANCE of HIS -

- PRESENCE - Deuteronomy 31:8; Isaiah 43:2; Matthew 28:20

- GRACE - Romans 3:23-24; 2 Corinthians 12:9; Ephesians 4:7

- PROTECTION - 2 Kings 6:17; Psalm 34:7; Psalm 91:1

- PEACE - John 14:27; John 16:33; Philippians 4:7

- VICTORY - Isaiah 65:17; Romans 8:28-30; 2 Corinthians 2:14

Trials are to be expected. They are part of life. To take up the cross and follow Jesus means suffering. Without it we cannot identify with Jesus.

When and where are we going to get some suffering time? We did not suffer before we came here, and we are not going to suffer in heaven. This short life span on this planet provides our boot camp.

March 24

TO CULTIVATE VIRTUES

- *LOVE* - Keep your heart open for God's love to flow through you to others. Be aware of any blockages like resentment, pride and self-centeredness.

- *JOY* - Praise God everywhere and for everything.

- *PEACE* - Keep your eyes on Jesus.

- *PATIENCE* - Stop for repairs on your attitude.

- *GENTLENESS* - Replace tension with soothing moments. (Music, nature, guided imagery, meditation).

- *INTEGRITY* - Obey the Word.

- *FAITHFULNESS* - Commitment to God, others and the task at hand.

- *HUMILITY* - Compare yourself to Jesus, not to others.

- *SELF-CONTROL* - Discipline the body by diet, exercise and rest.

Other virtues - Compassion, responsibility, friendship, work, honesty, loyalty.

March 25

NUGGETS OF WISDOM

Whatever happens to me has God's hand on it. He gives light in darkness, peace in turmoil, strength in weakness and love when no one cares.

Life is a process and a journey, not a product or a destination. Live for the moment with eternity in view, so you will honor the Lord in everything you do.

Hell is Truth seen too late. Hell is a place of remembrance - " *IF ONLY* ...."

Truth is not a concept to be studied, but a PERSON to relate to.

Christ-likeness is not "self" camouflaged in religious activities, but an attitude that flows from the very life of Christ as He indwells the believer.

Christianity is not a form of self-improvement; it requires that "self" be crucified.

March 26

FOUNDATION OF FAITH

GOD - as - Sovereign Creator. Genesis 1:1; Isaiah 44:24; Jeremiah 32:17
Righteous Judge. Psalm 145:17; Romans 2:2; Acts 17:31
Unconditional Love. Isaiah 54:10; Jeremiah 31:3; Romans 5:8

CHRIST - as - God's Son. Matthew 17:5; John 9:35-37; 20:31
Sin Bearer for man. Isaiah 53:5; 2 Corinthians 5:21; 1 Peter 3:18
Only way to God. John 14:6; Acts 4:12; Romans 5:12

HOLY SPIRIT - as - Third Person of the Trinity. Matthew 4:1; 28:19; 1 Peter 4:14
Teacher. John 14:26; Luke 12:11-12; 1 Corinthians 2:10-12
Resident in Christians. John 14:16-17; 1 Cor 6:19; Eph 4:30

WORD - as - Inerrant Truth. Psalm 19:7-8; Psalm 119; Romans 7:12
God inspired Truth. Acts 1:16; 2 Timothy 3:16; 2 Peter 1:21;
Unchanging Truth. Psalm 119:89; Matthew 5:18; 1 Peter1:25;

March 27

DEFIANCE AGAINST GOD

- Contempt for God's holiness.
- Indifference to God's love.
- Denial of Christ's deity.
- Rejection of His atonement for sin.
- Rebellion against His claim as the only access to God.
- Ignorance of the deity of the Holy Spirit.
- Disobedience for His guidance.
- Refusal to let Him take up residence within.
- Attack against the inerrancy of Scripture.
- Challenge the inspiration from God.
- Changing the Truth by interpretation, adding and subtracting.

TO BELIEVE IN GOD - To acknowledge that God exists. Even demons do this.

TO BELIEVE GOD - To accept everything God has said about Himself, His Son, the Holy Spirit, the Scriptures, creation, mankind, the history of the past, the state of the present, the events of the future, sin and redemption.

March 28

SECULAR VERSUS SPIRITUAL VALUES

Four elements the world considers essential for a happy life.

- Physical health for the body.
- Mental health for the soul.
- Education for the mind.
- Material wealth for satisfaction and status.

Four elements God considers essential for a joyous life.

- Hope - The healing of the body is guaranteed either here or in the thereafter.
    Isaiah 53:5; Malachi 4:2
- Love - Healing for the soul comes by the assurance of God's everlasting love.
    Jeremiah 31:3; 1 John 3:1
- Faith - Spiritual discernment leads to wisdom, far above the knowledge of
    this world. John 8:32; 1 Corinthians 1:18-31
- Gratitude - Contentment with God's grace.
    2 Cointhians 12:9; Philippians 4:11, 13, 19; 1 Timothy 6:6-8

March 29

ABANDONMENT TO GOD

In order for God to use us, we have to surrender all personal rights, power, strength, talents, mind will and emotions to Him. It is not what we do for God that is important, but our love and devotion to Christ. It is the work that God does through us that counts. When we are rightly related to God, we are in the right place at the right time.

It is by our reactions to the circumstances around us that determines whether we fail or fulfill God's purpose for us.

God does not always deliver us from bad situations, but He lets us experience His presence, love, light and peace. Faith is the unshakable trust in God's goodness, regardless of the circumstances. It will be tested to the limit time and again.

We have to be comfortable with the way things are, be ready for changes, be unperturbed by adversity and be imitators of the life of Christ.

God's plan for us might not involve any great accomplishment in this world, but a relationship with Him that surpasses the greatest joy.

Your value and worth comes from being a child of God, not from what you achieve.

The chief end of man is to glorify God and to enjoy Him forever.

March 30

QUESTIONS - ANSWERS

Questions from an unbeliever:

- Is God the creator of the universe?
- Who is Jesus Christ?
- What was and is His mission?
- Do we have direct access to God?
- Is the Bible history, philosophy or a fairy tale?
- What is the Holy Spirit?
- What is grace?

Answers from a believer:

- God created every thing in detail, not just the first cell of life.
- Jesus Christ is the only Son of God, the second Person of the Trinity. He is not some great teacher to show us how to live.
- Jesus Christ came to reconcile the depravity of man to the holiness of God, by dying a substitutionary death for our sins. He rose again in victory.
- God decreed the plan of salvation. There is only ONE way to God - through the Lord Jesus Christ.
- The Bible is the inerrant, inspired Word of God, not a mere account of human witnesses and interpretations.
- The Holy Spirit is the third Person of the Trinity, not a legend or a dream.
- Grace is not a favor of God to reward us, but a gift we don't deserve.

March 31

CHRIST'S MISSION

When Christ became man, He :

ABANDONED a sovereign position.
  ACCEPTED the place of a servant.
    APPROACHED a sinful people.
      ADOPTED a humble posture.
        ATONED for our sins.
          ASCENDED as a supreme Prince.

April 1

RESULTS OF SIN

The reason everything is out of whack in this life -

CAUSE - Disobedience. Genesis 3:1-6; Jeremiah 2:19; John 3:19

CONSEQUENCES -
* Depravity. (It fills our jails.)
  Genesis 6:5; Isaiah 1:6; 64:6; Romans 1:28-32; 3:23; 1 John 1:8
* Disease. (It fills our hospitals.)
  Genesis 3:16-19; 2 Chronicles 21:12-15
* Death. (It fills our cemeteries.)
  Ezekiel 18:4; Romans 5:1; 6:23

CURE - Jesus Christ.
* Savior by His atonement for us.
  Isaiah 53:5-6; Acts 4:12; 2 Corinthians 5:21
* Shepherd for our daily needs.
  Psalm 23; Isaiah 40:11; John 10:11
* Conqueror over all evil.
  John 16:33; 1 Cointhians 15:24-28; 1 John 3:8

April 2

THINGS TO THINK ABOUT

How you live your life is a testimony of what you believe about God.
Obedience is the outward expression of your love for God.
Prayer isn't a time to give orders, but to report for duty.
God does not function like a vending machine that delivers the candy we select when
    depositing a coin.
God's gift to me is my need to depend on Him.
Death is not a dead-end, but a fork in the road.
Contentment is an attitude we learn and a choice we make.
We cannot control the wind, but we can adjust the sails.
The Garden of Eden story proves that man, in a world without suffering, chose to seek a
    life without God's rules.
Without the bread of affliction, our souls would die of spiritual malnutrition.
The symphony God is working out includes minor chords, dissonance and lengthy fugal
    passages. But those who follow His conducting through these early practice sessions,
    will someday burst into a jubilant song with renewed strength.

April 3

ENERGY

The body, soul and spirit of each person contains a data bank to store information, energy, power and vitality.

How to waste power and lose energy

- Unforgiveness - Holding grudges, dwelling on the negatives.
  Power goes out into the past and contaminates the present.
  The immune system weakens.
- Self-Centeredness - Pride, self pity.
  Power is imprisoned and becomes a stagnant Dead Sea.
  A breeding ground for illnesses.
- Worry - Fear, unbelief.
  Power goes out into the future and becomes useless.
  The nervous system breaks down.

How to restore power and turn it into energy

- Identify the leaks.
- Ask "WHY" only in transit, while you assemble the repair kit.
- Take full responsibility for repairing the leaks. Plug them up with Scripture verses by submission, trust and obedience.

April 4

AGING

QUESTION - Why does God let us get old and weak?

ANSWER - Maybe God has intended that the strength and beauty of youth be of a physical nature. The strength and beauty of old age, however, can only be seen by spiritual discernment.
We gradually loose our youthful appearance that is temporary, so we can shift our focus on what is eternal. This will prepare us to leave the fleeting, deteriorating part of us and look forward to our glorified bodies.

If we stayed young, strong and beautiful, we might never want to leave this world !!!

April 5

TO STAY ON COURSE

Necessary attitudes for growing in Christ to spiritual maturity. 1. Peter 5:6-10

- Submission to the chain of command in families, government, authorities and God.
- Humility to serve others.
- Trust in God's sovereign purpose.
- Self-control in moral decisions.
- Vigilance over our enemies, the World, the Flesh and the Devil.
- Hope for God's best in the future often involves some pain in the present. Afterwards He will restore you and make you strong, firm and secure.
- Worship. If you surround yourself with praise, you don't question the difficulties of life. Nothing is beyond His control.

April 6

FROM DUSK TO DAWN

THANKSGIVING - <u>SUNSET</u>
> Giving thanks for what God has done in the past.
>> *PRAISE* - <u>NIGHT</u>
>> Utter trust in the goodness of God in the midst of darkness.
>>> *WORSHIP* - <u>SUNRISE</u>
>>> Overwhelming awe at God's omniscience, omnipotence, omnipresence, holiness and love.

April 7

WHY KEEP GOING?

When life feels like a treadmill of futility - remember -

- God's invitation to you is to enjoy His fellowship and learn more about Him.
- God's goal is to prepare you for heaven.
- God knows your life from beginning to end. He is using both successes and failures, health and sickness, happiness and sorrow to transform you into the image of His Son, Jesus Christ.

April 8

DISCIPLINE

External steps for a disciplined life.

- Unclutter your environment.
- Begin with small changes.
- Make an agenda.
- Be on time.
- Keep your word.
- Do the difficult tasks first.
- Finish what you start.
- Practice self-denial.
- Be flexible when disruptions occur.

Internal principles.

- Remember Who owns you. 1 Corinthians 6:19-20
- Remember the covenant of your salvation. Exodus 24:8; Hebrews 9:19-22
    Your part - Confession, repentance, obedience.
    God's part - Forgiveness, reinstatement, intimate relationship.
- Remember to monitor your thought life. Genesis 6:5; Matthew 15:19; James 1:14
- Remember that sin is a violation of an intimate relationship. Matt 23:37; Eph 4:30
- Remember to bring God glory and honor. Ps 86:8-12; 1 Cor 10:31; 1 Tim 6:15-16

April 9

DAVID

"A man after God's own heart."
Acts 13:22

- He had a deep yearning for the Presence of God. Psalm 27:4; 42:1-2

- He lived with a great zest for life. 2 Samuel 6:14-16; Psalm 108:1-4

- He was quick to confess his sins from the heart and repent genuinely.
    Psalm 32:5; 51:3-4

- He humbly accepted the consequences of his actions.
    2 Samuel 12:15-20; 1 Chronicles 28:2-6

April 10

A SEA JOURNEY

<u>GOD</u> - is our final destination.

        <u>CHRIST</u> - is our compass.

                <u>HOLY SPIRIT</u> - is our radar.

                        <u>SCRIPTURES</u> - are our charts and maps.

Christianity includes the compass, the radar, the charts and maps.
Liberalism dismisses the charts and maps.
Fundamentalism ignores the radar.
Humanism throws out the compass, radar, charts and maps.
Religion replaces the compass, radar, charts and maps with anything other than
        <u>Christ</u>, the <u>Holy Spirit</u> and the <u>Scripture.</u>

April 11

IN LINE

When the sun is vertically above us, we cast no shadows. Similarly, when we place ourselves under the Divine Meridian, our carnal shadow, which is the projection of self, will vanish. We will be in line with the Light.

What is the object of your meditation? Do you spend time thinking about Jesus and His love for you? Or are you only focused on your needs and desires? God's grace and mercies are vast. Our entire life is held together by the power of God. Therefore, let's take time to meditate on His goodness and personal care for us.

EVIDENCES OF BEING IN LINE

To be saved. Romans 10:9

      To be spirit-filled. Acts 13:52

           To be self-sacrificing. Luke 9:23

                  To be submissive. 1 Peter 2:13-14

                        To be sanctified. 2 Timothy 2:21

                              To be suffering. 2 Timothy 3:12

                                    To be grateful. 1 Thessalonians 5:18

                                    To be joyful. Philippians 4:4

TODAY was in God's mind long before the earth was created.

We don't know what the future holds, but we know *WHO* holds the future.

April 12

WAYS TO DEAL WITH CONFLICTS

- Aggression - To declare war. Matthew 26:52
- Revenge - To get even. Romans 12:19
- Withdrawal - To shrink back. Luke 9:59-62
- Denial - To pretend everything is OK. 1 Thessalonians 5:6-8
- Surrender - To give in. Ephesians 6:13
- Compromise - To meet half-way. 2 Corinthians 6:14-17
- Diplomacy - To address an issue face to face, and bring up something that needs to be resolved. Matthew 18:15-17
- Release - To hand the person and the problem over to God. 1 Peter 2:23

Revenge is natural; forgiveness is spiritual.
Getting even is the rule of the jungle.
Giving grace is the rule of the Kingdom.

April 13

RED FLAGS

Warning signs, alarms, monitors, gauges and indicators are manifested in the -

PHYSICAL BODY - as discomfort, pain and terminal illness.
SOUL - as discontentment, unforgiveness and depression.
SPIRIT - as guilt, indifference and death.

Take red flags seriously. Amos 4:9; Luke 16:28-31; Revelation 16:9-11
Seek help while it is available. Isaiah 55:6; 2 Corinthians 6:2; Hebrews 3:7-8

April 14

THE TEMPTATIONS OF JESUS

BODY -   Turn stones into bread. Instant gratification.
SOUL -   Throw yourself off the temple.
              Display your power for others to see.
              Use God for your own glory.
SPIRIT -   Grab the power, possessions and prestige of this world.
              Follow Satan, the god of this age, and you can have it all.

April 15

TWO QUESTIONS

Suffering involves two main issues : Who caused my adversity?

What is my response?

Apart from my own personal sins, I have no control over <u>who</u> is responsible for this terrible thing that has happened to me. But I have a choice of how to respond.

Let's turn from focusing on the "whys" of life to the one Who is in control. My adversity can become God's greatest gift to me, if it leads me to total dependence on Him.

Jesus kept the wounds of His humanity so He could continue to understand the needs of those who suffer.

God has two plans for accomplishing His goal.

PLAN <u>A</u>   He wants us to see the Truth in the Word and respond in faith and obedience.
             But because of the fall of man, God had to resort to

PLAN <u>B</u>   He has to allow some adversity into our lives, so we will learn to depend on
             Him. He has to jerk the rug from under our self-sufficiency.

April 16

GOD'S LOVE

<u>God has</u> -

*   Chosen you before the foundation of the world.
*   Predestined you to adoption into His family through His Son.
*   Unconditionally accepted you as His beloved child.
*   Redeemed you.
*   Forgiven all your sins --- past, present and future.
*   Desired to favor you abundantly.
*   Prepared an eternal heritage or you.
*   Sealed you for the day of redemption.

When we walk to the edge of the light we have and take that step into the darkness, we must believe that one of two things will happen:

There will be something solid for us to stand on

OR

We will be taught to fly.

April 17

SPIRITUAL GROWTH

The signs that we are heading in the right direction.

- A hunger to know God on an intimate level.
- An increasing awareness of our sins.
- Sincere repentance and a desire to become more Christ-like.
- To view spiritual battles, trials, temptations and failures as avenues of growth instead of obstacles.
- A desire to be used by God in the lives of others.
- A commitment to godly obedience.
- An increasing faith.
- A yearning to please God.
- A hunger for private devotion and prayer.
- An increasing awareness of God's presence.

April 18

OF FAITH, JOY AND PRAISE

The most important issue is not the amount of faith, but the object of our faith.

A good leader knows the way, shows the way and goes the way. There is never a time when God is not active in your life. So it is important to do what He says and believe what He promises.

When our faith fails, praise is the direct route to reestablish it.

Suppose that you will never receive an ounce of worldly recognition. Would you still enjoy life? When you have your eyes focused on Jesus Christ, He Himself becomes the source of your joy.

The secret of praise is not found in waiting until every thing in your life is peaceful and at ease. It is learning to praise God in the most difficult moments.

This is the greatest test of faith.

Requirements for praise -

Repentance of known sins.

Submission to God.

Absence of a critical spirit.

Confrontation with fear.

Gratitude for the way things are.

April 19

LIVING WATERS
John 7:38

The wellspring of life. John 4:14

Once a stream leaves it's source, it will encounter numerous obstacles. Where will the water go? If the power is sufficient at the source, the water will find a way around, over, under or through the blockages to spread it's life-giving essence, which is righteousness, peace and joy. Romans 14:17

Never focus on the obstacles, difficulties or temptations, but instead keep your eyes on the Source of all power, God, Jesus, the Holy Spirit and the Word.

April 20

THREE POINT GUIDELINE

- *ATTITUDE* - Give thanks for the freedom to choose whether to react or respond to a problem.

- *ACCEPTANCE* - Trust the sovereignty of God who allows both joy and sorrow to come your way. He will provide peace, joy and contentment to accept the things we cannot change.

- *ACTION* - Obey the Holy Spirit. He will provide the guidance, courage and strength to change the things we can.

When feeling unhappy, unappreciated, unfulfilled, unfit, unsure, unknown or
"UN –ANYTHING"
don't allow irritation, discouragement and self-pity to poison your soul.
Instead learn to give thanks.

Everything can be taken from man except one thing:
The last of the human freedoms -
To choose one's attitude in any given set of circumstances.

April 21

14 TIPS FROM ROMANS 14

- Keep caring, but give others the freedom to fail.
- Stay connected, but don't control others.
- Allow others to learn from natural consequences.
- Admit you are powerless; the outcome is not in your hands.
- Change yourself, not others.
- Be supportive, but don't "fix" others.
- Let others deal with the consequences; don't manipulate.
- Allow others to face reality; don't protect.
- Accept imperfection; don't live in denial.
- Search out your own shortcomings and correct them. Don't nag, scold or argue.
- Take each day as it comes. Don't insist on your rights.
- Become what you can be. Don't criticize others.
- Live in the present for the future, not in the past.
- Fear less and love more.

April 22

FROM THE ORCHARD

What does it mean to bear fruit ? John 15:1-8

- To develop a Christ-like character. Ephesians 4:24
- To display the Fruit of the Spirit. Galatians 5:22
- To be active in good works. Ephesians 2:10
- To be grateful. Hebrews 13:15

How does God prune us ?

- By allowing irritations, pain and sorrow in our lives. He prunes away those branches that <u>react,</u> in order to enable the others to <u>respond.</u>
- By applying the discipline of a loving Father.
- By helping us to understand and implement His Word.
- By opening our eyes to His creation and inviting us to praise and worship Him.

We have all eternity to celebrate our victories,
but only a short time before sunset
to win them.

April 23

WHAT WE NEED

Faith declares -

GOD was with me yesterday.

GOD is with me today.

GOD will be with me tomorrow.

I can do all things through Christ, who gives me strength.

If God in His love gives us opportunities to mature in our faith, we should face each problem with joy. We can learn to patiently and persistently declare that in each and every situation He is working all things for our good. We have only one thing to do :

To please Him.

Nothing, absolutely nothing can happen without His knowledge. Our faith in His control eliminates all kinds of fear.

The body reacts to what we believe. Let's learn to trust God in little things every day, <u>before</u> some great danger confronts us. Now is the time to rejoice and believe that God is using good or bad to bless me. What I am experiencing is exactly what I need at the moment. If I need the spiritual exercise of dealing with an irritable person, God will send that person to me. If we believe that God will take a problem and make it work for our good, God will use His awesome power to reward our trust in Him.

It is difficult to be upset about anything, if we really believe

that God is working for our good.

April 24

THEN AND NOW

Before the fall, the key requirement was <u>obedience.</u>

Adam and Eve had direct spiritual, mental and physical fellowship with God. They knew exactly God's assignment for them each day. There was no "dark night of the soul."

After the fall, the key requirement is <u>faith.</u>

In today's fallen world, the fellowship with God is severed by the depravity of man's spirit, the derangement of his mind and the physical limitations of his body.

Revelation 3:20 says : "Listen! I stand at the door and knock. If anyone hears

my voice and opens the door, I will come in and fellowship with him."

How does He knock? In the joys and sorrows of life. Every trial gives us the opportunity

to open the door for Christ to enter and help us. He is patiently waiting.

Let us turn to Him.

April 25

A TWO WAY STREET

Our way to communicate with God.

- Address the right God with reverence.
- Confess sins and repent.
- Give thanks for past blessings.
- Make specific requests.
- Intercede for others.
- Claim God's promises.
- Focus on Jesus. Obey God's Word. Yield to the Holy Spirit.

God's way to communicate with us.

- Through nature. It inspires the awe, praise and worship of the Creator. Rom 1:20-23
- Through music. Caution: Chain of command – melody, harmony, rhythm.
- Through the written Word. It focuses on the holiness and love of God.
- Through prayer. Verbalizing specific requests and waiting for the answers.
- Through Jesus Christ. He reveals God in human flesh.
- Through conscience. Caution: Does the information come from the Holy Spirit, self, the world, the flesh or the devil?
- Through personal revelation. Caution: Discern the source. 2 Corinthians 11:14

April 26

MUSINGS

What goes around, comes around.
    Whenever all seems lost, it isn't.
        When no one seems to notice, someone does.
            When everything seems great, it isn't.
                When nothing seems just, it is.
                    When God seems absent, He is present.

Without Christ we are not ready to die.
    With Christ we have everything we need to live or die.
Reputation is what other people think of you.
    Character is what you are in the dark, when no one is watching.
People mistake sex for love, money for brains, TV for civilization, morals as a matter of taste, life as a racket, religion as a mechanism for escape, man as a glorified gorilla and God as a vending machine.

April 27

SEVEN DOWN - SEVEN UP

STEPS IN THE WRONG DIRECTION -

Entrance of a questionable thought.
      Entertainment of the thought.
            Examination of the thought.
                 Enjoyment of the thought.
                      Excuse for the thought.
                            Enactment of the thought.
                                 Enslavement by Satan.

STEPS BACK TO WHOLENESS -

                      Conviction.
                  Confession.
              Repentance.
           Separation.
        Submission.
      Forgiveness.
Vigilance.

April 28

WHY THE TREE ?

<u>The Tree of the Knowledge of Good and Evil.</u> Genesis 2:9,16-17; 3:1-7

The fruit of the tree was not poison, but the disobedience to a specific command of God was. Man traded the godly wisdom for human knowledge and personal experience of good and evil. Now man alone is responsible for his choices based on his own understanding.

The intimate relationship with God was severed, and man was left to his own devices.

Disobeying God brought on the *experimental* knowledge of good and evil, which is
                happiness and misery, joy and sorrow.

      Righteousness is the result of Christ's atonement for our sins.
      Holiness is the result of the choices we make in obedience to the Trinity.

April 29

PROBLEM SOLVING STEPS

- *CONFESSION* - Get in tune with God. Psalm 66:18; Proverbs 28:9; Micah 3:4
- *FAITH* - Believe in the Holy Trinity. Hebrews 11:1,6; 1 John 5:4
- *PRAYER* - Be specific and persistent. Matthew 7:7; John 15:7; James 1:5; 4:2
  Listen carefully. 1 Kings 19:12; Isaiah 30:21
- *ACTION* - Obey the revealed will of God. Jeremiah 7:23; Luke 6:46;   John 14:15
- *PRAISE* - Give thanks in advance. Psalm 43:5; John 11:41-42; Philippians 4:6
- *TESTIMONY* - Share the victory with others. Psalm 107:21; Luke 8:39

April 30

WORTH NOTING

We can learn brevity from Jesus. His greatest sermon can be heard in eight minutes. His best known story can be read in ninety seconds. He summarized prayer in five phrases.
He silenced accusers with one challenge. He rescued a soul with one sentence. He condensed the Law in three verses. He reduced all His teachings to one command.

If our greatest need had been information, God would have sent an educator.
If our greatest need had been technology, He would have sent a scientist.
If our greatest need had been money, He would have sent an economist.
If our greatest need had been physical health, He would have sent a doctor.
If our greatest need had been protection, He would have sent a policeman.
But since our greatest need is forgiveness,
God sent a Savior.

There is more to life than meets the eye. That is where faith comes in. Faith is trusting what the eye cannot see. Eyes see the prowling lion; faith sees Daniel's Angel. Eyes see storms; faith sees Noah's rainbow. Eyes see giants; faith sees the Promised Land.

Unhappiness on earth cultivates a hunger for Heaven. The only tragedy is to seek satisfaction in the temporary things of this world, apart from God's will. It is to settle for a "bowl of soup." To feel at home in a strange land. To mix with the Babylonians and forget Jerusalem. To despair in the moment and lose sight of eternity.

May 1

SURVIVAL

<u>S</u> - Surrender all "If Onlys."
       For sins - confess and repent. 1 John 1:9
       For bad choices - accept the consequences. Luke 15:18-19

<u>U</u> - Understand the sovereignty, holiness and love of God.
       Study His Word. 2 Timothy 3:16
       Search out His will. Psalm 143:10; Romans 12:2

<u>R</u> - Remember past blessings. 1 Samuel 7:12; 12:24; Psalm 103:1-2

<u>V</u> - View the problems from God's perspective. Isaiah 55:8-9; 2 Peter 3:8

<u>I</u> - Intercede for others. Job 42:10; Matthew 5:44

<u>V</u> - Validate your feelings. Don't suppress emotions. Zechariah 7:11; Matthew 13:15

<u>A</u> - Accept your daily assignment. Matthew 16:24; Luke 5:4-5

<u>L</u> - Lean on God's grace. 2 Corinthians 4:15-18; 12:9

May 2

LORD, BLESS MY ENEMIES

When someone makes you angry, bitter or resentful, there is a powerful remedy:
Think of some wonderful blessing that God could bestow on that person who angered you, and then steadfastly pray that He will do so. This way, you are pleasing God, defeating the enemy and receiving a joyful heart.

Lower your expectations of people. This is not Heaven, so don't expect it to be. There will never be a newscast without bad news. There will never be a church without gossip or strife. There will never be a new house, a new spouse, a new career, a new hobby that can give you the joy your heart craves.

Earth is not what we had hoped for. Something inside us groans for more. Endurance and patience will be rewarded. If you must pay a price, pay it. No sacrifice is too much. If you must leave the baggage on the trail, leave it. No loss will compare to what is in store.
Whatever it takes --- do it!

May 3

IF GOD IS ....

- If God is sovereign, I can relax. Proverbs 16:33; Isaiah 45:5-7; Daniel 4:35
- If God is faithful, I can trust Him. Psalm 143:8; 1 Peter 4:19
- If God is holy, I want to worship Him. Psalm 99:9; Isaiah 6:1-3
- If God loves me, I want to obey Him. Jeremiah 31:3; John 14:15
- If God is omniscient, I don't need to know everything. Deut 29:29; Job 33:13
- If God is omnipresent, I don't need to fear. Psalm 139:7-11; Deuteronomy 31:8
- If God is just, justice will prevail. Deuteronomy 32:4; Revelation 15:3-4

May 4

PARENTING

Proverbs 22:6 "Teach a child how he should live, and he will remember it all his life."

If you have done your very best in bringing up your children, this verse gives you a promise you can hold on to when the children are out of God's will.

On the other hand, this same verse becomes an accusation when you know you have failed as a parent. We cannot ease the concern for our children by worrying about them, but we *CAN* release them into the sovereign, holy and loving hands of God.

To be a parent can be a fulfillment, a joy, a struggle, a frustration, a nagging pain, an overwhelming defeat or a never-ending nightmare.

The joy of parenthood is a privilege, never a right. If I have claimed it as my right, I must relinquish it. If things go wrong, approach your Heavenly Father and hand Him your broken toy. "With God, all things are possible." Mark 10:27

May 5

HEAVY LOAD

Never attempt to bear more than one kind of trouble. Some people carry three loads:
The trouble they had in the past.
>The trouble they have now.
>>The trouble they expect in the future.
We lose the joy of living in the present,
>when we stew about the past and
>>worry about the future.

May 6

SERVANTHOOD

"I am not here to be served, but to help others." Mark 10:45; John 13:14-17

Self-centeredness is at the bottom of fights in the nursery, arguments at school, tensions between people and war among nations.

Self-centeredness is the root cause of pride, discouragement, irritation, unforgiveness, depression, hostility and rage.

Life turns sour when our feelings, our dignity, our rights, our talents, our gifts, our position and our importance are misunderstood, criticized, ignored or discarded.

When we focus, dwell or concentrate on our unmet emotional needs, it is a sure sign that we are out of sync with God.

There is a remedy: Remember your job description -
*   To walk with Jesus.
*   To praise God.
*   To obey the Holy Spirit.

When self dies - Jesus lives!

May 7

RANDOM THOUGHTS

What God permits, He also uses redemptively. Will <u>we</u> permit what <u>God</u> permits?

We pray: "Lord, get me out of this mess."

But the Lord replies: "Let me <u>into</u> your mess. Permit me to change <u>you</u> rather than change your circumstances."

The only power Satan has are his lies and getting us to believe them.

Our testimony is threefold: Who we are (our character), what we do (our conduct) and what we say (our words).

Happiness comes from what happens - joy comes from our relationship with God.

Problems are opportunities to discover God's solutions.

Why is the world in such a mess? The leaders have tossed out the instruction book.

Sow a thought - reap an action.

Sow an action - reap a habit.

Sow a habit - reap a character.

Sow a character - reap a destiny.

May 8

THE ESSENCE OF HOPE

- Jesus didn't remain a baby. Luke 1:80
- Our crucified Savior did not remain in the grave. Matthew 28:1-7; Revelation 1:18
- Our risen Lord did not remain on the earth. John 14:2; Acts 1:9
- Our ascended Lord won't remain in heaven. John 14:3; Acts 1:10-11
- Our glorified Lord will reign forever. Revelation 11:15-17

May 9

TWELVE VIRTUES

Prayer.	Luke 18:1; 1 Thessalonians 5:17
Forgiveness.	Luke 23:34; Colossians 3:12-13
Honesty.	Psalm 15:1-2; Zechariah 8:16-17; Luke 16:10
Integrity.	Daniel 6:4; Revelation 14:5
Self-discipline.	Romans 13:14; 1 Corinthians 6:12
Humility.	Micah 6:8; Philippians 2:3
Gratefulness.	Psalm 34:1; Ephesians 5:20; 1 Thessalonians 5:18
Kindness.	John 13:34; Ephesians 4:32;
Compassion.	Matthew 9:36; Luke 10:33-34
Loyalty.	Matthew 6:24; 1 Corinthians 4:2
Patience.	Psalm 40:1; Hebrews 10:36
Endurance.	Galatians 6:9; James 1:12

May 10

TO COMMUNICATE

If you agree - affirm it.

If you disagree - speak up.

If you don't understand - ask questions.

If you have other ideas - share them.

If you have nothing to say - give a hug.

God has chosen the way of prayer to interact with us. It is the secret code to connect us to Him and from there to reach others. Prayer knows no limits.

May 11

THE WILL OF GOD

- God's universal Will. *THE LOGOS* - His Will as revealed in the Bible.
- God's intentional Will. *THE RHEMA* - In one way or another, we have all missed the boat, blown the opportunity, disobeyed the inner voice or lost our way.
- God's circumstantial Will. Through His Son, Jesus Christ, He applied His mercy, forgiveness and grace and glued the broken pieces of our lives together again.
- God's immediate Will. He sent the Holy Spirit to guide us in our walk with Him.

Seven ways to check out if we are in the will of God -

Is it consistent with His Word?
> Can I in earnest ask for God's help?
>> Does the Holy Spirit within agree?
>>> Is this in harmony with who I am?
>>>> Will it help me to grow spiritually?
>>>>> Will it benefit others?
>>>>>> Will it bring glory to God?

May 12

IN A NUTSHELL
Proverbs 4:23-27

- Guard your soul. Proverbs 23:7; Matthew 26:27
- Guard your mouth. Psalm 39:1; Matthew 12:36; James 3:5
- Focus on your goal. Deuteronomy 5:32; Philippians 3:13
- Plan ahead. Matthew 6:20; Romans 13:14
- Hang in there. Galatians 6:9; Hebrews 12:1
- Avoid evil. 1 Thessalonians 5:22; James 4:7

STRUGGLES with self -
> *STRUGGLES* with others -
>> *STRUGGLES* with the world system -

Faith in the Cross makes all difficulties to work FOR you. That includes whatever -

God does.
Satan is allowed to do.
Other people do.
You do.

May 13

BASIC HUMAN NEEDS

- *SELF-WORTH* through acceptance and belonging.
    Damaged by shame and rejection.
- *SECURITY* through food, clothes, shelter, light.
    Damaged by abandonment.
- *STROKES* through affection from family and friends.
    Damaged by neglect or abuse.
- *STRUCTURE* through boundaries and predictability.
    Damaged by indifference or chaos.
- *STIMULATION* through fun and challenges.
    Damaged by guilt or unrealistic expectations.
- *SELF-ACTUALIZATION* through permission to be unique and different.
    Damaged by criticism and condemnation.
- *SPIRITUALIZATION* through finding truth, purpose and meaning in life.
    Damaged by "religions", orthodoxy or liberalism.

May 14

ARE PETS SAVED ?

Three reasons why I believe animals have eternal life -

- God brought the animals into the Ark to save them from judgment.
    Genesis 6:18-21
- God promises to redeem His creation and deliver it from bondage.
    Romans 8:18-25
- Some animals have the capacity to love, and love is eternal.
    Luke 7:47; 1 Corinthians 13:13; 1 John 4:16

Death is not the extinguishing of the light.
It is merely switching off the lamp,
because the dawn has come.

May 15

ATTITUDES

Life is 10 % what happens to us and 90 % how we respond to it. We always have the power to choose our attitude.

When all the strings on my instrument break, I can still play a melody of praise on ONE string -- my attitude.

Attitude is more important than education, money, health, success, prestige, power and comfort.

There are four strings : *Health, Riches, Relationships, Attitude.*

We spend more time concentrating and fretting over the strings that snap, dangle and pop (the strings that cannot be changed), than focusing on the one that remains - attitude.

We have four choices :

- *The Worry-wart* -   We waste time and energy on things beyond our control. We <u>contaminate</u> our environment.
- *The Blame-game* -   An aggressive attitude reacts to circumstances with resentment and anger by blaming God, Satan, fate and others. We <u>explode</u> outwards.
- *The Pity-party* -   A passive attitude sends us to a self-imposed prison. We <u>implode</u> inwards.
- *The Victory-lane* -   The choice to stay on TOP with trust, obedience and praise. <u>Practice, practice, practice !!!</u>

The choice of my attitude and actions I make today, determines the memories I will have of yesterday, and the rewards I will reap tomorrow.

God can weave the thorns of life into a crown of glory.
Matthew 5:11-12; Romans 8:18, 28; 2 Corinthians 4:16-18; 1 Peter 1:3-9

May 16

GODLINESS

Godliness is an attitude deep down below the surface of life.
A heart that is sensitive towards God and takes Him seriously.
One who hungers and thirsts after God.
One who listens to Him, wants to know Him and walks with Him.

Psalm 42:1-2; Psalm 63:1; Psalm 84:2

May 17

NOW AND THEN

One of these days we are going to look back on the brief life we have lived down here where we have suffered so many afflictions. Then we will go to God and thank Him for every problem, every disappointment, every faithless friend, every heartache and every false accusation that ever has been made against us.

We will say :"Oh God, I thank you for putting me on the operating table and cutting out that which was hindering me in my walk with you. I now know that I have been trained and prepared for the eternal glory in your presence."

Abiding in Christ means to sit at the feet of Jesus with an obedient heart. It is walking in unbroken communion with the Lord. It means wanting to live life His way. His thoughts and His ways become my thoughts and my ways. To do that, I have to give up my own agenda for my life.

When we are born, we are given a "car" to drive down the highway of life. When we are saved, we stop the car and pick up Jesus. But He is only a passenger in the back seat until we deliberately turn the steering wheel over to Him to be in control.

May 18

T O P

Three ways to stay on TOP of the *"world"*, the *"flesh"* and the *"devil."*

TRUST the Sovereignty of God when navigating the unpredictable waters of the world.
         Isaiah 55:8-9; Matthew 14:24-33; Mark 5:36
     My commitment - Psalm 56:3-4; Proverbs 3:5-6; 2 Corinthians 5:7
     God's response - Deuteronomy 31:8; Joshua 1:9; Isaiah 41:10, 13

OBEY the Holiness of God by staying on course during the temptation of the flesh.
         Jeremiah 7:23; 38:20; Luke 6:46
     My commitment - Joshua 22:5; Luke 10:27; 2 Corinthians 5:9
     God's response - Deuteronomy 11:26-28; 28:1-2; 1 Samuel 15:22-23

PRAISE the Love of God by resting in the eye of the storm of Satan.
         Isaiah 26:3-4; Psalm 46:1-11; Mathew 8:23-27
     My commitment - Psalm 34:1; 103:1-2; Habakkuk 3:17-18
     God's response - Psalm 22:3-5; Isaiah 61:3; Hebrews 13:8

God's pledge to know us is backed up by His Omniscience.
God's pledge to help us is backed up by His Omnipotence.
God's pledge to be with us is backed up by His Omnipresence.

May 19

TO MEET WITH GOD

Requirements for approaching God - *MAKE PREPARATIONS.*

- Segment of time. Make an appointment to meet with God.
- Seclusion. Select a place where you can be alone.
- Self-control. Make this meeting the top priority of the day.
- Stillness. Meet first thing in the morning, before the clamor and clutter set in.
- Silence. Be patient in waiting for God to reveal Himself.
- Sensitivity. Adjust and tune your soul to God's frequency.
- Submission. Make a conscious choice to obey.

How to approach God - *HAVE A PLAN.*

- Review your past. Confess your sins, repent (turn around, make amends), accept
    forgiveness, learn from your experience, focus ahead.
- Reflect on God. Who He is and what He had done. Visit with Jesus.
    Listen to the Holy Spirit.
- Remember God's promises. Hold on to them for encouragement.
- Request a clear understanding of His will and agenda for you.
- Render thanks for the privilege for having access to the Trinity.

May 20

SEEING HIM

"Oh God, our Lord, your name is wonderful everywhere on earth." Psalm 8:9

Not today, but some day, God will be worshipped on all the earth. In our time, we live in a universe that is groaning, travailing in pain, waiting for the redemption. (Romans 8:22).
But God is above all creation. He has set His glory above the heavens. And up yonder is that Man who two thousand years ago came down to this earth to be born in Bethlehem.
He is seated now in glory at God's right hand. Only by faith are we able to see Him.

"All of us then, reflect the glory of the Lord with uncovered faces; and the same glory, coming from the Lord, who is the Spirit, transforms us into the likeness in an ever greater degree of glory." 2 Corinthians 3:18

What a glorious prospect this is for the child of God.

ANTIDOTES

WORRY, ANXIETY, FEAR -
>   Jesus in the Garden of Gethsemane. Luke 22:44

- Identify your concern.
- Lay it on the altar. 2 Chronicles 20:12; Psalm 55:22; Isaiah 41:10;
>   2 Timothy 1:12; Hebrews 4:16
- Rest on God's perfect love, infinite wisdom and absolute control.
- Walk hand in hand with Jesus.

REJECTION, LONELINESS, DEPRESSION -
>   Jesus suffered the ultimate loneliness. Matthew 27:46

- Identify the problem.
- Connect with God. Jeremiah 29:12-14; 33:3
- Focus on bringing glory to God. 1 Corinthians 10:31; 2 Cor 5:9; Colossians 3:23-24
- Walk hand in hand with Jesus.

SHAME CONNECTED TO SIN -
>   Jesus took our sins unto Himself. 2 Corinthians 5:21

- God created everything perfectly. Genesis 1:31
- Take the shame to the Cross. Hebrews 12:2
- We can be clothed in His righteousness. 2 Corinthians 5:1-4; Revelation 3:18; 16:15
- God will redeem His creation. Isaiah 54:4-5; 65:17; Romans 8:18-25; Rev 21:4

DEFIANCE FOR GOD -
>   Jesus faced the utmost contempt of His deity. Matthew 27:28-31

- Identify the sin. Evolution, religion, cults, humanism, homosexuality, rebellion.
- Take a firm stand for God. Deuteronomy 30:19; Joshua 24:15, 22-24;
>   1 Kings 18:21; Psalm 119:30
- Release the problem to God. Deut 32:35; Psalm 10:1-18; 12:1-5; 37:1-2; 52:1-7;
>   Psalm 94:1-11; Micah 5:15; Nahum 1:2-3
- Pray to bring good out of evil. Genesis 50:20; Matthew 6:9-10; Romans 8:28

May 22

BI-POLAR

In order for a musical instrument to sound nice, the strings have to be tuned to the perfect pitch. In a spiritual sense, that is the wave-length of God.

Problems either prevent the necessary tension on the "strings" of our souls, or they can stretch us uncomfortably.

In *DEPRESSION,* the strings lack tension and are out of tune.
In *MANIA,* the strings are too tight and are equally out of tune.

To tackle both problems, start by giving thanks to God for His presence. As the strings adjust to God's pitch (His perspective), we are able to praise Him for Who He is.

Up from depression, this brings *JOY* to life.
                    Down from mania, this brings *PEACE* to life.
                                        The music in our soul will bring *LOVE* to life.

May 23

THOUGHTS CREATE EMOTIONS

Comparison to a water purifying plant.

The source of the water - people, circumstances, environment.
The filter - attitudes, perception, thoughts in the mind.
The bucket - emotions fill it with pure or contaminated water.

- To identify the source. Negative thoughts can become magnified in the mind,
                    overloading the filter. Put closure to it by forgiveness.
- To empty the bucket of feelings. Expressing frustrations, disappointments
                    and fears by confessing, forgiving, talking to God.
                    Unless we turn the negative faucet off, the tank will
                    fill up again.
- To install a "Border Guard". Filter every thought before granting entrance to
                    the mind by asking:

                    Is it true ?
                              Is it in line with the Word ?
                                        Is it compatible with Jesus ?
                                                  Will it bring glory to God ?

WHAT ARE BOUNDARIES ?

They are not walls, but doors we can open or close. Before we can establish boundaries, we have to know who we are and where we are. The land has to be owned first.

EXAMPLES OF BOUNDARIES -
>Words (yes or no).
>>Personal convictions.
>>>Geographical locations.
>>>>Time limits.
>>>>>Emotional space.
>>>>>>Spiritual guidelines.

WHAT IS INSIDE OUR BOUNDARIES -
>Feelings.
>>Attitudes.
>>>Behaviors.
>>>>Choices.
>>>>>Values.
>>>>>>Abilities.
>>>>>>>Will.

BOUNDARY PROBLEMS -
>Compliance: To say yes to what is not good.
>>Pessimism: To say no to what may be good.
>>>Domination: To ignore the boundaries of others.
>>>>Denial: To avoid getting involved.

PRINCIPLES GOVERNING BOUNDARIES -
>Know your motives.
>>Consider the consequences.
>>>Take responsibility for your choices.
>>>>Respect the other party
>>>>>Be flexible.
>>>>>>Be honest.
>>>>>>>Be guided by love.

RESISTANCE TO BOUNDARIES -
>Criticism and anger from others.
>>Guilt messages from others.
>>>Insecurity.
>>>>Fear of rejection.
>>>>>Misunderstandings.

QUALIFICATIONS FOR HAVING BOUNDARIES -
>Care about others without trying to "fix" them.
>>Listen, but don't analyze, except when asked.
>>>Allow feelings to be expressed.
>>>>Tell the truth in love.

May 25

WHAT TO TEACH CHILDREN

These ten concepts are the most important.

* The unfailing truth of Scripture.
* To know God's sovereignty, holiness and love.
* To know Jesus Christ as a sin-bearer and a personal Friend.
* To know the Holy Spirit as a teacher, guide and helper.
* How to be saved.
* Who they are - unique, important and loved.
* Why they are here - to honor God by trust, obedience and praise.
* To appreciate creation and be good stewards of the environment.
* The principle of sowing and reaping - consequences of attitudes and actions.
* Their ultimate accountability to God.

> The decisions they make determine the quality of their lives today,
> and the rewards or regrets they will experience tomorrow.

May 26

THE LIMITATIONS OF MONEY

MONEY CAN BUY -

A house, but not a *home.*
Food, but not an *appetite.*
Comfort, but not *rest.*
A bed, but not *sleep.*
A college education, but not *wisdom.*
Medicine, but not *health*
Material things, but not *contentment.*
Leisure, but not *fulfillment.*
A legal settlement, but not *peace.*
Entertainment, but not *happiness*
A caretaker, but not a *friend.*
A crucifix, but not a *Savior.*
A good life, but not *eternal life.*

Wealth is an attitude of contentment, inner peace and a steady walk with God.
Remember where you came from and where you are going. Job 1:21; Luke 12:16-21
Invest in lasting values. Isaiah 55:2; Matthew 6:19-21; John 6:27

NON-NEGOTIABLE DOCTRINES

- *TRINITY* - God the Father, God the Son, God the Holy Spirit. One God in three
      manifestations and functions.
          Matthew 3:16-17; 28:19; John 14:26; 15:26; 2 Corinthians 13:14.

- *GOD* - Creator of the universe. Genesis 1:1-27. Infinitely holy. 1 Pet 1:16.
      Loving. Jer 31:3; John 3:16. Just. Deut 32:4. Omniscient. Psalm 139;1-4.
      Omnipotent Jer 32:27; Mark 10:27. Omnipresent. Prov 15:3; Jer 23:24.
      Sovereign. Daniel 4:35; 1 Timothy 6:15-16.

- *CHRIST* - Virgin born. Luke 1:35. Son of God. Matthew 17:5.
      Redeemer of mankind. John 1:29; 14:6; 1 John 3:5.
      His Death and resurrection. Romans 10:9; 14:9.

- *HOLY SPIRIT* - Indwells believers for guidance and comfort. John 14:16-18, 26.
      Intercedes for believers. Romans 8:26-27.

- *SCRIPTURES* - God's Word contains everything necessary for this life.
      Psalm 119; Luke 16:29; 2 Timothy 3:15-17;
      2 Peter 1:19-21; Revelation 22:18-19.

- *DEPRAVITY OF MAN* - Genesis 6:5; Isaiah 1:5-6; 64:6-7; Jeremiah 17:9, 23;
      John 3:19; Romans 1:18-32; 3:10-18.

- *SALVATION* - By faith alone. Galatians 3:11. In the finished atonement of Christ.
      Galatians 2:21; Ephesians 2:8-9; Titus 3:5.
      For good works. Ephesians 2:10; James 1:22; 2:26; 4:17.

- *LIFE AFTER DEATH* - Luke 16:22-26; Hebrews 9:27.
      With God. John 14:1-4; 2 Corinthians 5:6-10; Rev 21:3-7.
      Without God. Revelation 20:11-15; 21:8.

NOT ALONE

The upheavals of life become the workshop to practice our faith in the sovereignty, holiness and love of God. They challenge us to leave our boats of security and walk on the water. Faith does not eliminate the storms, but gives us strength to cope with them.
When we look what the world did to Jesus, we should not expect exemption from suffering. But He has gone before us to prepare the way and be with us.

May 29

BEWARE !

Don't seek counsel from people who -

Are not role models.

          Are unbelievers.

                Don't mention God.

                      Don't offer prayers.

                             Contradict God's Word.

                             Have a seared conscience.

                      Support ungodly life styles.

                Charge a big fee.

          Place personal happiness over concerns for others.

Gain control by making you "co-dependent".

May 30

THREE TYPES OF CALLS

- *GENERAL* - To all people to be converted. 1 Timothy 2:4

- *DISCIPLESHIP* - To all Christians to surrender personal rights. Luke 9:23

- *SPECIAL* - Individuals who are hand picked for specific tasks. Matthew 22:14
        Examples : Abraham, Moses, Elisha, Isaiah, Jeremiah, Paul.

May 31

HANG IN THERE !

Life may not always turn out the way you had planned, but ultimately God will be glorified and you will be blessed.
- Recall past victories.
- Examine your attitude.
- Recognize the true nature of the battle.
- Focus on God - not your problem.

Our heart is like a crooked fence. All the paint in the world won't straighten it out.
Integrity is not wrapped in a prayer shawl, but it is Christ likeness in work clothes.
The Grace of God greases the frictions of life. 2 Corinthians 12:9

June 1

INTERACTIONS

- *ACQUAINTANCE* - To know certain things <u>about</u> a person, but not the person himself.
- *SYMPATHY* - Superficial understanding of someone's temporary emotion.
- *AFFINITY* - Soul mates who are on similar wavelengths concerning specific interests, goals and activities.
- *FRIENDSHIP* - To <u>know</u> a person intimately, heart to heart.
- *EMPATHY* - Desire and commitment to get to know a person on an intimate level, by correctly understanding his personality, motives, actions, feelings and emotions. Finding out what makes a person tick and where he is coming from.
- *COMPASSION* - Empathy with the desire to help. Insights that are followed by actions.

June 2

THE SUFFICIENCY OF GRACE

God's provision for salvation, sanctification and glorification is enough -

He has removed the *PENALTY* of sin.
He offers continuing *POWER* over sin.
He will abolish the very *PRESENCE* of sin.

God's provision is manifested in -

REDEMPTION. Ephesians 1:7
RENEWAL. 2 Corinthians 4:16
REWARD. Revelation 22:12

PAST (Night) - the penalty of sin is paid.
PRESENT (Dawn) - the power over sin is available.
FUTURE (Day) - the presence of sin is annihilated.

Prelude - Outer Court.
Interlude - Holy Place.
Postlude - Holy of Holies.

June 3

HOW FAITH WORKS

Being a child of God, walking hand in hand with Jesus and being guided by the Holy Spirit, do not always protect us from disappointments, rejection, injustice, sorrow, pain, hardship, illness, suffering and trauma, because we live in a fallen world under the dominion of Satan. Isaiah 14:16-17; Ephesians 6:12
But we have the assurance that the Presence of God will be with us and in us in the

midst of

the fiery furnace Daniel 3:25
        the lion's den Daniel 6:22
                the water and the fire Isaiah 43:2
                        the battles 2 Kings 6:17; 2 Chronicles 20:15
                                the daily struggles Deuteronomy 31:6

June 4

THREE LEVELS OF FAITH

WEAK FAITH - lacks two things -
        Comprehension of who God is. Romans 1:19
        Commitment to follow Him. Matthew 13:19-22

MATURE FAITH - the gift God gives us in response to our comprehension and
        commitment Our spirit and the Holy Spirit click to be on God's wave-length,
        in harmony with His plan and in step with His activities. The foundation is laid
        to build on. 1 Corinthians 3:11. The soil is prepared for the seeds. Matthew 13:23

AUTHORITIVE FAITH - our response to God's call for –
        Evangelism Matthew 28:19-20
                Witness Matthew 5:13-16
                        Compassion Luke 10:33
                                Service Matthew 20:26-28
                                      Intercession Ps 106:23; Ezekiel 22:30

To move from weak, sporadic and strong faith to <u>unshakable</u> faith -

- Learn all you can about the object of your faith, God, by studying His Word.
- Obey and apply what you have learned.
- Observe how God responds to your reaching out to Him.
- God can make a way when there is no way. He will never leave you nor forsake you.

June 5

INTERCESSION FOR LEADERS

We should pray for -

- Conviction, confession, conversion, comprehension, commitment.
- Submission to God for wisdom, courage and strength.
- Clear guidance on what is best for the nation.
- Personal integrity.
- Awareness of the accountability to God for attitudes, motives and actions.
- *That God's will be done, regardless of the weaknesses and mistakes of those in authority.*

Wisdom is the Fruit produced by the Mind through knowledge of all the facts; by the Body through experience gained by turning head knowledge into actions, an abstract idea into a concrete form, and by the Spirit through understanding, discernment, interpretation and divine guidance.

June 6

UNDER ATTACK

- *DISHARMONY* - Relationships that are out of tune, painful and derailed.
- *DISCONTENTMENT* - Self-pity.
- *DISCOURAGEMENT* - When the focus is on the problem instead of God's solution.
- *DEFEAT* - Failure to transform and overcome.
- *DOUBTS* - Questions about God's goodness.
- *DIVERSION* - Filling needs in other ways than God's.

FOCUS ON

- *PRAISE* - Daniel 3:17-18; Habakkuk 3:17-18
- *PROMISES* - Isaiah 61:3; Romans 8:18
- *PRIZE* - Imperishable Crown. 1 Corinthians 9:25
  Crown of righteousness. 2 Timothy 4:7-8
  Crown of life. James 1:12
  Crown of glory. 1 Peter 5:4

June 7

MOTIVATIONS FOR PRAYING

- Desire for God to be glorified.
- Desire for fellowship with God.
- Desire to express gratitude for past, present and future blessings.
- Desire for mercy and grace.
- Desire for needs to be met.
- Desire for guidance, discernment and wisdom.
- Desire for deliverance from oppression.
- Desire for the salvation of the lost.
- Desire for the sanctification of believers.
- Desire for God's will to prevail.
- Desire for the return of the Lord Jesus Christ.

June 8

A LIFE OF PRAYER

WHEN TO PRAY -

When guilty - confess, repent, reconnect.
When forgiven - intercede for others.
When sick - seek the prayers of others.
When happy - give thanks.
When sad - pour out your heart.
When desperate - praise and worship.

WHEN THOUGHTS WANDER -

Recite what you have memorized.
Focus on a specific prayer object.
Pray over whatever comes to mind.

ENEMIES OF PRAYER -

Doubts - Is God really loving and trustworthy?
Fear - What if God lets me down?
Distractions - Enticing voices clamor for our attention.
Priorities - Any activity we would rather do.

June 9

HARD WORK

Praying is like climbing up a steep mountain. Fatigue and discouragement can set in.

- Get in tune with God. Seek His presence. Do penance. Render petitions. Praise.
- Resist the lure of comfort in food, sleep or distractions.
- Resist the temptation to quit.
- Be prepared to wait.
- Scan the horizon for answered prayers, however small.
- Continue to give thanks for the results God has chosen.

June 10

BOGGED DOWN

When our prayer life is drowning in the -

Rivers of relationships that are strained, lukewarm, critical and unforgiving.
Lagoons of loneliness in a prison, on an island or on the sidelines.
Waters of worry that poison our faith.

June 11

BEHIND THE SCENES

Life is an accumulation of single pictures. God can connect these individual events so they become a continuous motion picture that runs it's course until it finally comes to "The End."

God's love, purpose and involvement give understanding, meaning and hope to our lives. Each biography is different, but the ultimate goal is the same - to be conformed to the image of Christ and give glory to God.

When frustrations over people and events tempt us to cut up the film and toss some pictures out, we break the cycle of blessings until repairs are made in form of confession, submission, forgiveness, thanksgiving and praise. Once we see each event of our lives as part of God's plan for us, we realize that every episode is important and can be worked for our good.

June 12

MY HEART'S DESIRE

- To meet with Jesus face to face every morning for encouragement and instruction on what to be, think and do.
- To walk hand in hand with Him through the day.
- To receive an evaluation, correction and forgiveness every evening.
- To be filled with the Holy Spirit and under the protection of God's perfect love, infinite wisdom and absolute control for 24 hours, 7 days a week.

June 13

CAUSES OF DEPRESSION

Repressed anger.

Deep sense of shame.

Inability to give and receive love.

Lack of opportunity to express compassion.

Rejection from family and friends.

Elusive guidance on what to do.

Unrealistic expectations

Blocked creativity

Isolation.

June 14

HELP ALONG THE WAY

GOD'S PROMISES -

Deuteronomy 31:8; 2 Chronicles 20:15; Psalms 32:8; 55:22; 119:105; Psalm 145:18-20; Isaiah 41:10; Jeremiah 31:3; 33:3; John 14:27; Romans 8:28; 1 Corinthians 2:9; Revelation 21:4

GOD'S PROVISIONS -

His written Word.
The Holy Spirit. 1 Kings 19:12; Isaiah 30:21; John 14:16-18; Romans 8:26
Other people - books, radio messages, personal contacts. Acts 2:42
Sovereign miracles. John 9:1-7; 11:4

June 15

WHO ARE WE ?

TEMPERAMENT - Inherited genetic make-up. The raw material we have to work with.
Parable of the talents. Matthew 25:14-30

CHARACTER - The result of the natural temperament molded by family, environment,
education, challenges, successes and failures. Mind, will, emotions.
Proverbs 23:7; Matthew 15:18-19

PERSONALITY - Outward expression of a genuine or faked character.
1 Samuel 16:7

SPIRITUAL TRANSFORMATION - The soul yields control to the Holy Spirit.
Romans 12:2; 2 Corinthians 5:17

June 16

THE FOUR TEMPERAMENTS

SANGUINE - Lives in the present. Enjoys today. Forgets the past. Is optimistic.
Psalms 118:24; 100; 150; John 2:1-10; 15:11; Romans 12:15
Example - David, Peter.

CHOLERIC - Takes action. Welcomes challenges. Positive leadership. Fearless.
Daniel 3:16-18; Acts 27:21-26; Philippians 3:13-14
Example - Paul.

MELANCHOLIC - Sensitive, perfectionist, faithful, loyal, dependable, compassionate.
Psalms 27:4; 73:25-26; Matthew 23:37; Mark 1:35; Luke 10:42
Example - Moses, Elijah.

PHLEGMATIC - Calm, cool, collected. Practical thinker. Dry humor. Peacemaker.
Genesis 13:8-9; Matthew 5:9; Romans 12:16-18
Example - Abraham.

The *hard-driving Choleric* produces and carries out the inventions of the *genius-prone Melancholic,* which are being marketed by the *personable Sanguine* and enjoyed by the *easy-going Phlegmatic.*

TWO KINDS OF LIFE

View life on this earth as a preparation, education, boot camp and maturing process.
Romans 8:17-18; 2 Corinthians 4:16-18; 1 Peter 1:6-7; 4:12-13

LIFE ON EARTH -	*LIFE IN HEAVEN -*
Human love. (Eros, Philia, Storge)	God's love. (Agape)
Happy	Joyful
Contentious	Peaceful
Frustrating	Fulfilled
Dissonant	Harmonious
Selfish	Generous
Adrift	Anchored
Prideful	Serving
Enslaved	Free
Short	Eternal
Contaminated	Purified
Painful	Blissful
Overwhelming	Challenging
Scary	Safe
Lacking	Satisfying
Discouraging	Uplifting
Obscure	Enlightened
Stressful	Soothing
Hectic	Relaxed
Superficial	Profound
Restricted	Unlimited
Lonely	Connected

When going through suffering, don't look at what is seen, but what is not seen; for the former will pass away, but the latter will last forever. 1 Peter 5:10

- God will perfect us (correct, adjust, align, restore).
- God will establish us (to be confident, steadfast, unwavering).
- God will strengthen our faith.
- God will set us on an unshakable foundation.

June 18

WHAT'S IN STORE

In the life to come, the grace of God allows us to share in the glory of Christ, which is -

- A *LOVE* that cannot be fathomed.
- A *LIFE* that cannot end.
- A *RIGHTEOUSNESS* that cannot be tarnished.
- A *PEACE* that cannot be explained.
- A *REST* that cannot be disturbed.
- A *JOY* that cannot be diminished.
- A *HOPE* that cannot be disappointed.
- A *MESSAGE* that cannot be misunderstood.
- A *CONNECTION* that cannot be broken.
- A *STRENGTH* that cannot be weakened.
- A *PURITY* that cannot be defiled.
- A *BEAUTY* that cannot be marred.
- A *LIGHT* that cannot be extinguished.
- A *TRUST* that cannot be betrayed.

June 19

THE PURPOSE OF THE LAW

The Word of God reveals that man is a sinner in need of a Savior.
The Law is like a mirror. It has no cleansing power. It only shows that we are dirty.
We can refuse to look in the mirror or even break it, but that does not change the fact that we are unclean in God's eyes.
The Law never made man a sinner, but it revealed the fact that man was, is and will be a sinner until cloaked with the righteousness of Jesus Christ.

The Blood of Christ is the Cleansing Agent for our sins.

Consider Mr. Nice, the pleasant, thoughtful, helpful, generous non-Christian. It is difficult to think of such a person as sinful and in need of regeneration. But sin is not defined in terms of what a human outwardly appears or what he does or does not do.
Neither is our society a measuring stick of what is good or evil. Sin is first and foremost a failure to love, honor and obey God. Thus, even the likable and law-abiding person is in need of a rebirth as much as any obnoxious, crude and decadent criminal.

There is no salvation in good works, only in the vicarious death and resurrection of
JESUS CHRIST.

June 20

WHAT PEOPLE ASK

QUESTION - Why do bad things happen to good people?
ANSWER - They don't.
EXPLANATION - There are no good people.
                Psalm 53:2-3; Proverbs 20:9; Ecclesiastes 7:20; Romans 3:10-12

QUESTION - Why do bad things happen to righteous Christians?
ANSWER - They don't.
EXPLANATION - The tragedies will be changed into triumphs, the pain into blessings,
                the losses into rewards. Genesis 50:20; Psalm 30:5; Romans 8:28

QUESTION - Why do good things happen to bad people?
ANSWER - They don't.
EXPLANATION - The good is only temporary. Justice is coming.
                Psalms 37:1,35-38; 73:3-17; Proverbs 24:19-20; Amos 6:1-8;
                Luke 6:24-26

June 21

SOME THINGS TO THINK ABOUT

Don't plan to repent at the 11th hour - you may die at 10:30 !

Peace is not dependent on the ending of the storm. It is determined by our awareness of the presence of Jesus Christ in the midst of the storm.

Worry is an old man bent over carrying a load of feathers which he thinks is lead.

How you live your life is a testimony of what you believe about God.

Truth is not a concept to be studied, but a Person to relate to.

To believe in God is to acknowledge that God exists. Mark 1:24; 5:7; Luke 4:34, 41
To believe God is to believe everything He has said about Himself, His Son, His creation,
        the past, present, future, sin and redemption. Genesis 1:1; Isaiah 45:5; John 3:16;
        Hebrews 9:22; Revelation 22:13

Before you talk to God about your depressed soul, talk to your depressed soul about God.

To have faith in God is to always be thankful to Him, to accept and obey His will, to discern His goodness behind every circumstance and to have a heart ready to praise Him.

June 22

22 PILLS

These 22 "pills" can transform your attitudes. They are in alphabetical order to make it easier to memorize. They will heal damaged relationships and help you to like people better. Eventually, the Holy Spirit will enable you to love them.

ACCEPTANCE - discrimination
  BENEVOLENCE - ill-will
    COMPASSION - complacency
      DIALOGUE - monologue
        ENCOURAGEMENT - low self-esteem
          FORGIVENESS - bitterness
            GENTLENESS - irritation
              HONESTY - deceit
                INTERCESSION - indifference
                  KINDNESS - rudeness
                    LOYALTY - betrayal
                  MERCY - vengeance
                NURTURANCE - neglect
              OPENNESS - secrecy
            PATIENCE - frustration
          QUALITY time - distractions
        RESPECT - contempt
      SACRIFICE - selfishness
    THANKFULNESS - criticism
   UNDERSTANDING - narrow-mindedness
 VIRTUE - immorality
WILLINGNESS - reluctance

June 23

GIVING THANKS

An attitude of gratitude is giving thanks <u>FOR</u> everything. Ephesians 5:20

A proof of faith is giving thanks <u>IN</u> everything. 1 Thessalonians 5:18

A sacrifice of praise is giving thanks <u>BEYOND</u> everything. Hebrews 13:15

June 24

DIALOGUE

Have you ever written a letter to someone in which you really opened your heart? You probably have felt vulnerable as you waited for a response. When the long awaited letter finally came, there was not one word that in any way connected to anything you have written. It ignored everything you have said, but mentioned only issues the other person was interested in.

The Bible is God's personal Letter to us. In it He opens His heart to communicate the way, the truth and the life that bring us back to Him, so we can fully experience His presence and His love. We can respond by trust, obedience, praise and eagerness to get to know Him better, or we can ignore Him and center our attention only on our own self.

Don't break hearts by rejecting an offer for friendship.

June 25

THE BENEFITS OF SUFFERING

- Suffering drives to prayer. Psalms 18:4-6; 120:1; 130:1-2; 142:1-2; Jonah 2:2
- Suffering teaches patience. Romans 5:3; James 1:2-3
- Suffering releases God's power. 2 Corinthians 12:9-12; 13:4
- Suffering enhances productivity. John 15:1-2
- Suffering promotes perseverance. Revelation 2:7, 17, 26
- Suffering develops compassion. 2 Corinthians 1:3-7; Hebrews 4:15
- Suffering prepares for purity. 1 Peter 5:10
- Suffering ultimately leads to praise. Romans 8:18

I cry: "Lord, I need a way out !!! I feel like a bird in a cage. I am totally depressed."
The Lord answers: "But even a bird in a cage can sing."

- God is in control. Isaiah 45:5-7
- He is working everything for my good. Romans 8:28
- I have only ONE thing to do - PLEASE HIM. 2 Corinthians 5:9

The good news is not that Jesus lived and died;
but
that He died and lives.

June 26

"UN"-ANSWERED PRAYERS

I asked for health, that I might do greater things -
    I was given infirmity that I might do better things.
I asked God for strength that I might achieve -
    I was made weak that I might learn to obey.
I asked for riches that I might be happy -
    I was given poverty that I might be wise.
I asked for power and the praise of men -
    I was given weakness to sense my need of God.
I asked for all things that I might enjoy life -
    I was given life that I might enjoy all things.
I got nothing I asked for but everything I hoped for -
    In spite of myself, my prayers were answered.
I am among all men most richly blessed.

June 27

WHAT IS BETTER ?

We can pray for -

Possessions
    Power
        Pleasures
            Promotions
                Prominence
                    Popularity

<u>OR</u>

A PASSPORT TO HEAVEN
John 14:6

Complacency - Resignation to our fate without a motivation to change things.

<u>OR</u>

CONTENTMENT - Finding joy wherever we are without any resentment over our past
        or present situation.

June 28

LIVING IN DIFFERENT TIME ZONES

When we are wandering in times not our own, we ruin our todays by mixing spoiled yesterdays or unripe tomorrows into a stew.

Some people live with yesterday's slights, grudges and guilt. Something bad happened to them and they can't forget it.

Others live with tomorrow's threats, evil and sorrows. Something fearful might happen to them, and they worry that they might not be able to cope with it.

God divided life into bite-size chunks of time, called days. Trying to chew more than one at the time can choke us.

God has promised to take care of us today. He can't help us with the future until we get there. And when we get there, it is no longer tomorrow, it is today.

Don't trip over anything that is behind you.

Brooding over the past rots the present and contaminates the future.

Anxiety does not empty tomorrow of it's sorrow, but it does empty today of it's joy.

"Maybe we should think only about today," says Lucy. Charley Brown disagrees: "No that is giving up. I'm still hoping that yesterday will get better." !?!

June 29

TODAY IS THE DAY

Now is the time to hear and act.
2 Corinthians 6:2; Ephesians 5:16; Colossians 4:5; Hebrews 3:15

There is no heartache, no pain, no darkness, no evil, no despair that cannot be lovingly touched by the God of all comfort. He, who has Himself suffered so greatly at the hands of men, will help, encourage, strengthen and guide you.

Because Christ has experienced the ridicule and rejection of men and now stands as our great High Priest, the Throne of Grace beckons every believer.

June 30

COMFORT

In the dark of the night - *the LIGHT OF LIFE* is with you.
In the midst of the storm - *the PRINCE OF PEACE* is your steadfast guide.
In the bottom of the pit - *the CHIEF CORNERSTONE* is your rock.

- Comfort for the body. Luke 10:33-34
- Encouragement for the soul. 2 Corinthians 1:4 1 Thessalonians 5:9-11
- Hope for the spirit. Ephesians 1:18; 1 Peter 3:15

LORD, I THANK YOU FOR ....

THE FATIGUE - that I may come to you for rest. Jeremiah 6:16; Matthew 11:28-30

THE WEAKNESS - that I may experience your strength. 2 Corinthians 12:10

THE DIFFICULT CIRCUMSTANCES - that drive me to your Word on how to respond
     in a Christ-like way.
     Jeremiah 33:3; Matthew 7:7-8; James 1:5; 1 Peter 2:21-23

THE BURDENS - that You are willing to carry for me.
     Psalm 55:22; 1 Peter 5:7

THE UNCERTAINTY - that teaches me to exercise
     faith 2 Corinthians 5:7 ,
     trust Psalm 37:5-7; Proverbs 3:5-6; Isaiah 55:8-9,
     patience Lamentations 3:25-26; Hosea 12:6; James 1:3

THE DISAPPOINTMENTS - through which I may see that nothing can change your
     love and plan. Jeremiah 29:11; Romans 8:28; Philippians 1:6

THE TRIALS and TEMPTATIONS - that give me opportunities to be a witness for You.
     Job 1:21-22; 2 Corinthians 4:8-11; 6:3-10

THE DISCOURAGEMENTS - that I may look for the "Promised Land."
     Deuteronomy 1:21; Isaiah 42:3; Mark 10:27

THE DEPRESSIONS - when nothing but your grace keeps me going.
     2 Corinthians 12:9

THE FAILURES - when you offer
     forgiveness Isaiah 43:25; 1 John 1:9,
     hope Hebrews 6:17-1
     a new start Lamentations 3:22

THE PHYSICAL and EMOTIONAL PAIN - that enables me to have compassion.
     2 Corinthians 1:4

THE UTTER HELPLESSNESS - that makes it impossible to function without you.
     Psalm 34:17-19; Isaiah 57:15; 66:2; Matthew 5:3; John 15:5

July 2

THE PROCESS OF SANCTIFICATION

We have the freedom to direct our attention to whatever we want to, but we also begin to resemble the object we dwell on.

At the time of salvation, we aim our "camera" on Christ and start taking pictures of Him as we see Him. The better we know Him, the better we can focus.

After the image is impressed on the "film", it must be developed in the "darkroom". The photo process requires darkness, right temperature, special chemicals and time to bring out the picture. Likewise we must go through affliction, trials and tribulation to mature us to be witnesses for Christ. 1 Peter 5:10; 6:7

Sanctification aims to produce a picture <u>in us</u> that resembles Christ.
Proverbs 4:18; Romans 8:29; 1 Corinthians 15:49; 2 Corinthians 3:18; 5:17;
Philippians 3:12; Colossians 3:3-4; 1 John 3:2-3

July 3

STAGES OF SPIRITUAL GROWTH

- *SALVATION* - Unconditional acceptance by God.
- *SERVICE* - A desire to serve God in any way He leads.
- *FRUSTRATING INADEQUACY* - Self-efforts, failures.
- *SPIRITUAL DEPENDENCY* - We turn to God for help. Some progress begins.
- *EXAMINATION of our MOTIVES* - Housecleaning by confession.
- *PAINFUL SURGERY* - Removal of deep-seated roots.
- *PEACE, FREEDOM and JOY* - The ultimate goal is no longer service but
CHRIST-LIKENESS

July 4

TO ABIDE IN CHRIST

An intimate relationship with Christ must be based on rock-bottom honesty. I must be free to express the whole gamut of emotions, positive and negative.

To abide in Christ does <u>not </u>mean to live a life of absolute obedience and perfection, but it is a walk with Christ towards perfection, while learning obedience one step at the time.

July 5

LOST CONTACT WITH GOD
Psalm 66:18; Isaiah 59:1-2

- To commit secret sins. John 3:19-20
- To have doubts. John 10:24-26
- To be defeated. Luke 22:61
- To do your own thing. Isaiah 53:6
- To be caught up in the world. 2 Corinthians 6:17
- To knowingly disobey. Deuteronomy 1:42-43
- To be distracted. Luke 10:41-42
- To entertain worldly thoughts. Jeremiah 4:14
- To hold a pity-party. Ecclesiastes 2:11
- To lose sight of life's purpose. Matthew 27:3-5

July 6

CONNECTED TO GOD
Psalm 24:3-5; 27:4

- To walk in the light. Psalm 89:15; Proverbs 28:13; 1 John 1:7
- To keep the feet on the rock. Psalm 40:2; Matt 7:24; 1 Corinthians 3:11; 1 Pet 2:6
- To stay under God's umbrella. Psalms 18:2; 34:7; 91:1-16; Proverbs 18:10
- To stay in the eye of the storm. Psalm 16:8; Isaiah 26:3
- To obey His commandments. Joshua 22:5; Luke 10:27; 1 John 3:24
- To heed the "Still, Small Voice." 1 Kings 19:11-12; Isaiah 30:21; Revelation 3:20
- To pray without ceasing. Luke 18:1; Ephesians 6:18; Philippians 4:4, 7, 11
- To focus on the ultimate goal - Christ-likeness. Romans 8:29; 1 Peter 1:13-16; 1 John 3:2

July 7

OLD AND NEW COVENANT

The old Covenant depended on obedience to an externally imposed Law. The new Covenant is written upon men's hearts. There is no longer the terror of punishment, but an invitation to respond to God's love. Believers choose to obey because they want to please God, not because the Law ordered them to do so.

The new Covenant is a love relationship, free of coercion and pressure.

July 8

BE PREPARED
Proverbs 4:23-27

- Guard your soul (mind, will, emotions). Your thoughts become actions.
    Proverbs 23:7; Matthew 12:33-37; 26:41
- Guard your mouth. Psalm 39:1.
    Monitor the words that come out. James 3:2
    Monitor the food that goes in. Proverbs 23:1
- Focus on your goal - T O P
    Trust. Proverbs 3:5-6; 2 Corinthians 5:7; 2 Timothy 1:12
    Obey. Joshua 22:5; Luke 6:46; 2 Corinthians 5:9
    Praise. Psalms 34:1; 103:1-3; Habakkuk 3:17-18
- Deploy the Scripture. Joshua 1:8; Ephesians 6:17; 2 Timothy 3:16-17
- Depend on the Savior. Jeremiah 17:7-8; Matthew 11:28-30; 1 John 4:4
- Hang in there. Job 17:9; Galatians 6:9; Hebrews 12:1
- Avoid evil. 1 Thessalonians 5:22

July 9

ROADBLOCKS AHEAD

How to face difficult and unpleasant situations.

- Consult the Lord and talk it over with Him. Jeremiah 33:3; Philippians 4:6
- Think in big dimensions. Keep the overview. Isaiah 55:8-9
- Approach the problem without anxiety. Matthew 6:34
- Share your burdens with the Lord. Psalm 55:22; 1 Peter 5:7
- Set priorities. Take one step at the time. Matthew 6:33
- Thank the Lord for the situation just as it is. Ephesians 5:20; 1 Thessalonians 5:18

July 10

THE MAKING OF A STRONGHOLD

A suggestion of Satan is allowed entrance into our soul.

It is nurtured and allowed to build a nest.

The snake, Satan, curls up in the nest to hypnotize the host.

July 11

TIPS FOR A HEALTHY RELATIONSHIP

- *ACCEPTANCE* - I am OK, you are OK. Matthew 7:1-5; Luke 10:27
- *RESPECT* - See the other as a person of value. Philippians 2:3
- *CONSIDERATION* - "Do unto others ......" Matthew 7:12
- *TRUST* - A step in faith. 1 Corinthians 13:7
- *VULNERABILITY* - Willingness to suffer. 2 Timothy 3:12
- *HONESTY* - Does truth prevail, or are games involved? Ephesians 4:25
- *COMMUNICATION* - Freedom to share and ask questions. James 5:16
- *FORGIVENESS* - Forgive others, as God has forgiven you. Matthew 6:14-15
- *COMPASSION* - Willingness to offer help. 2 Corinthians 1:4-5

July 12

GOD'S AMBULANCE

When I *fear*, He assures me. Proverbs 3:25-26; Isaiah 4:10

When I *fumble*, He directs me. Jeremiah 33:3; James 1:5-8

When I *falter*, He encourages me. Deuteronomy 31:8; Joshua 1:9

When I *faint*, He revives me. 1 Kings 19:4-8; Jonah 2:5-10; Mark 5:41-42

When I *fall*, He picks me up. Psalms 37:24; 40:1-2; Proverbs 24:16; Micah 7:7-8

When I *fail*, He provides a new start. Lamentations 3:23; Phil 3:13-14; 1 John 1:9

July 13

THE WAY, THE TRUTH AND THE LIFE.
John 14:6

THE WAY - Ask Jesus what He would do, if He were in my situation.

THE TRUTH - I would obey, if I truly believed in the warnings and promises of God's Word.

THE LIFE - I would always praise and worship, if I knew all the facts.

DIFFERENT WAYS TO DEAL WITH A CRISIS

This process can take anywhere from seconds to a lifetime.

- *DENIAL* - "Oh no !!!" State of shock, numbness, refusal to acknowledge reality,
  functioning like a robot, lethargy, feverish activities, too much sleep,
  loss of sleep, too much eating, or no eating.
  A built-in mechanism operates to screen out devastating information and to prevent
  us from becoming overloaded.
  Denial is a shock absorber for the soul. It is an instant and natural reaction to pain,
  loss and change. It protects us from the blows of life until we can gather up enough
  resources and strength to cope.

- *ANGER* - "No fair!!!" Frustration, irritation, indignation, wrath, fury, rage.
  It is a strong creative force that must be dealt with by either diffusion,
  expression, neutralization or sublimation.

- *BARGAINING* - "Wait a minute!!!" We make promises and vows to God if He
  would just fix the problem. When He doesn't, we attempt to prevent the
  inevitable and ease the pain with temporary remedies, like analgesics,
  pills, food, sleep or distractions. We try to solve the problem by our own strength.

- *DEPRESSION* - "No way out !!!" Our efforts have failed. We are exhausted
  from the struggle to ward off reality. We are stuck in a dark tunnel and feel the pain.

- *RESIGNATION* - "So what !!!" It is a passive and negative acceptance. We act
  as if everything is all right, when it isn't. We settle in the tunnel and lick our wounds.
  Denial, anger, bargaining and depression are still present, but we don't deal with
  them.

- *ACCEPTANCE* - "Thank you, Lord !!!" We get up, pick up the pieces and start walking towards
  the end of the tunnel. We realize that we have benefited from the crisis. We are content
  and at peace with our circumstances.
  Life is OK just the way it is right now.

"I LOVE YOU WITH AN EVERLASTING LOVE" Jeremiah 31:3

"MY GRACE IS SUFFICIENT FOR YOU" 2 Corinthians 12:9

"I WILL NEVER LEAVE YOU NOR FORSAKE YOU" Hebrews 13:5

PSALM 15

"Who shall abide in God's Tabernacle? Who shall dwell in His Holy Hill?"

<u>Answer</u> - The ones who adjust and correct their walk, work, words, way of response, will and wealth.

- *WALK - He who walks uprightly.*
    To walk in the Spirit. Galatians 5:16.
        Obedience to the guidance of the Holy Spirit.
    To walk in Faith. Hebrews 11:6
        To believe is to consent to something we have heard. To have faith is to
        act on something we know.
    To walk in Love. 1 John 4:7-8
        Love must flow in four directions – towards God, our immediate family,
        other believers, unbelievers and enemies.
    To walk in the Light. 1 John 1:7
        We must abandon every dark area of our life.

- *WORK - He who works righteously.*
    We must work <u>with</u> God (Mark 16:20), <u>unto</u> God (Acts 10:35) and
    <u>for</u> God (1 Corinthians 10:31).

- *WORDS - He who speaks the truth in his heart.*
    Conception - An idea enters the mind.
    Gestation - A thought develops in the womb of the soul. It activates the will
        and is nurtured by the emotions.
    Birth - The tongue brings forth the finished product.

- *WAY of RESPONSE - He who does no evil to others.*
    We lose contact with God when we harbor bitterness.

- *WILL - He who keeps his promises.*
    The mind gives the facts, the emotions provide the fuel, but it is the will that makes the
    decisions.

- *WEALTH - He who is generous and takes no bribes.*
    Our wealth must be honestly earned, wisely invested, carefully spent, generously given and
    diligently protected.

FROM CLASSROOM TO WORKPLACE

Imagine sitting in a school where the Apostle Paul teaches the basic doctrines of the Christian faith as presented in the first eleven chapters of the Epistle to the Romans.

Step by step he takes us through the reasons and methods God has provided to secure our salvation. It shows how to be reconnected to God and spend eternity in His presence. The bottom line is faith in the finished work of the Lord Jesus Christ. Our starving souls feed on all the words, blessings, assurances and promises that are presented to us. We are being carried to the lofty heights of the glory of God. Romans 11:33-36

But then comes Romans 12:1-2 !!!

"Since God has given us so much, let us offer ourselves as a living sacrifice to Him, dedicated to His service and pleasing Him. Let us not conform ourselves to the standards of this world, but let us be willing for God to transform us inwardly by a complete change of attitude. Then our whole life will be in line with His perfect will."

Now the time has come to put into practice what we have learned in the classroom. The emphasis shifts from what God has given us to what we can give back to Him.

How can we possibly match His extravagant mercy, grace and love? The only way is to present our whole being, spirit, soul and body voluntarily and unconditionally to Him.
This is NOT a one-time act, but a continuous commitment 24 hours a day, 7 days a week, motivated by a grateful heart.

Deuteronomy 6:5 *"We must love the Lord our God with all our spirit, soul and body."*

This is done in four ways - Deuteronomy 10:12-13

- To submit to God's requirement for salvation.
- To walk in His ways by holding fast the hand of Jesus.
- To serve Him by praise and worship.
- To obey the assignment He has given us.

Prayer corrects our attitude.

Praise affects our attitude.

Worship reflects our attitude.

July 17

EMOTIONS, GOOD OR BAD ?

Emotions can be described as "energy in motion." They can churn with love, hate, fear, anger, happiness, ambition, hunger, disgust, pain, frustration, loneliness, shame, guilt. When blocked or denied expression, they can become like a wild pack of dogs locked in a basement, where they multiply and tear the place up. It is not the traumas we suffered in childhood, which make us emotionally ill, but the inability to deal with them.

The attempt to numb the emotional pain is to create a time-bomb consisting of a growing accumulation of pent-up energies. The 12 Step meetings provide a safe environment for identifying and getting to know them and introducing them to light, freedom and love.

- *HEALTHY SHAME* - A God-given safety mechanism to protect against pride and guilt and remind us that we are human beings.
- *TOXIC SHAME* - A condemnation of our basic humanness by Satan, inflicted through other people, especially family and authority figures in childhood.
- *HEALTHY GUILT* - A God-given alert system that indicates that we have transgressed our boundaries set by God's Word.
- *TOXIC GUILT* - Condemnation of our actions by others.
- *ADDICTION* - Any attempt to dull the pain and escape reality.
- *CONTROL* - Using willpower and force to stop the upsetting behavior of others.
- *CRITICISM* - A subjective assessment of a person by self-righteousness.
- *FEEDBACK* - An objective and unbiased evaluation without a personal input.

July 18

THE ROLE OF THE SOUL

The soul is the home of the <u>mind</u>, the <u>will</u> and the <u>emotions</u>. In the spirit-filled soul, the mind must be in charge. The mind is the trainman, the will is the engine and the emotions are the cars. If the will receives instructions from any other source than the spirit-filled mind, it will run amok or the emotions take charge.

When we listen to our feelings, we may hear a whining voice: "Why me?" "I don't feel like it." Or an enticing voice: "Do it, it will make you feel good." Or an angry voice: "Get even – revenge yourself!" Invariably, we feel worse afterwards. The domino effect has started. Joy, peace integrity, self-esteem and hope get knocked down.

Emotions are like little children. They should be understood, loved, nurtured and guided, but they should not be allowed to rule our lives. We have limited control over our feelings, but maximum control over our choices and actions.

July 19

RECOVERY FROM DEPRESSION

- Determine the cause of the depression, whether it is spiritual, psychological or physical.
- Understand your feelings, but focus on your behavior.
- Avoid the sin trap. Remember the domino effect.
- Establish a specific plan of action.
- Be assertive. Don't let anger build up, but deal with it by expressing your feelings in an honest, loving and tactful way.
- Understand your motives. Beware of the "Helper Syndrome."
- Develop a friendship. A friend is someone who is concerned, interested, listening, understanding, sensitive, loving, accepting and open to share his own struggles and victories.
- Realize that there IS hope.
- Offer praise, no matter what.

July 20

RESPONSE TO AN OFFENSE

We cannot "give up" any feelings, because they are not volitional. A feeling is not a sin, but becomes one when acted out in ways contrary to God's Word. God puts away anger and bitterness <u>after</u> the offended person forgives the offender.
Forgiveness is an act of the will in which the believer turns the offenses over to God.
Letting an offender off the hook by excusing and rationalizing, is <u>not</u> forgiveness.

To reconfirm forgiveness in prayer -

- Tell God that you have forgiven the offender as an act of the <u>will.</u>
- Tell God that you know in your <u>mind</u> that you have forgiven the offender.
- Ask God to bring the <u>emotions</u> in line with your mind and will.
- Tell God that you know by His Word that He will deal personally with the offender.
- Ask God to remove any desire to retaliate.

Would you dig into yesterday's garbage to make tonight's meal? Then why do you dwell on an old offense to create today's experience? To blame others is one of the surest ways to stay in a problem, as we give away the very power and energy we could use to heal and restore ourselves. Whatever we focus on is energized to either hurt or bless us. When we are stuck and do not flow freely with life, we might be holding on to some feelings from the past. The basic cause of regret, fear, guilt, blame, resentment or anger is the state of unforgiveness, a refusal to let go and move on.

July 21

THE END PRODUCT

Every circumstance in life, every work, achievement, success as well as failure is nothing more than the scaffold, which forms the framework for building the real structure. It will be discarded in the end, when the permanent building is completed. Your soul, the individual <u>you</u>, is the artwork that will last forever.

Therefore focus your attention on maturing and getting closer to the goal, than on the means of getting there. When your chief desire is to glorify God, <u>everything</u> can become the means to achieve that end.

Tools for living that are only temporary -

- The physical body provides an abode and transportation for the soul.
- Money provides sustenance and security.
- Material possessions allow for comfort.
- Activities offer challenges, stimulation and pleasure.
- Jobs give opportunities to learn skills.
- Obstacles train for fitness.
- Pain tests the endurance.
- Various situations give a choice of attitudes.
- Time imposes discipline and patience.
- Adversities work on faith.
- Disappointments offer a workshop on hope.
- Relationships teach us how to love.

A TOMBSTONE EPITAPH

"End of construction. Thanks for your patience."

July 22

JUST FOR TODAY .....

Just for today, I will walk with Jesus.
> Just for today, I will obey the Holy Spirit.
>> Just for today, I will give thanks for past blessings.
>> Just for today, I will affirm life as it is.
>>> Just for today, I will praise God, no matter what.

July 23

A CONTRACT

WHAT I WANT TO DO FOR GOD -

To love Him. Luke 10:27
To thank, praise and worship Him.
   Ps 34:1; 61:8; 1 Thess 5:18
To please Him.
   2 Corinthians 5:9
To trust Him.
   Psalm 37:5; Proverbs 3:5
To abide in Him.
   John 15:7
To obey His Word.
   Joshua 22:5; John 14:23
To pray.
   Philippians 4:6; 1 Thess 5:17
To forgive others.
   Matthew 18:21-22
To be a blessing to others.
   Genesis 12:2
To run the race.
   1 Corinthians 9:24; Philippians 3:14
To be conformed to Christ.
   Philippians 2:5
To rejoice. Psalms 32:11; 37:4; 100:1-2
   Phil 4:4; 1 Thessalonians 5:16
To ask for a new heart.
   Ezekiel 11:19

WHAT GOD WANTS TO DO FOR ME -

To love me. Jeremiah 31:3
To let me experience His presence.
   Psalm 22;3
To please me.
   Luke 12:32; John 10:10
To guide me.
   Psalm 32:8; Proverbs 3:6
To protect me.
   Psalm 91:1
To keep me well.
   Deuteronomy 4:40
To respond.
   2 Chronicles 7:14-15; Psalm 91:15
To forgive me.
   Matthew 6:14
To bless me.
   Psalms 29:11; 128:1; Isaiah 44:3
To reward me.
   2 Timothy 4:8; James 1:12
To conform me to Christ.
   Romans 8:29
To provide mercy and grace.
   Psalms 23:6; 100:5; Hebrews 4:16
To give me my heart's desire.
   Psalm 37:4

July 24

OBEDIENCE PAYS OFF

- God's commandments do not imprison us or limit our potential.
   John 8:31-32; 10:10
- God wants us to be well, safe and useful.
   Deuteronomy 4:40; Joshua 1:8; Psalm 1:2-3; Proverbs 1:33;
- God wants to bless the future generations. Psalm 103:17-18
- God's perspective is higher than what we can understand. Isaiah 55:8-9
- God's ways and works are righteous and holy. Psalm 145:17
- God wants to give us hope and a future. Jeremiah 29:11
- God's ultimate goal for us is conformation to Christ. Romans 8:29-30
- God's motive behind all of His commandments, is love. Jeremiah 31:3

July 25

DON'T QUIT !

Getting ready for life's obstacle course -

- Assemble your gear.
    - Spirit - Put on the armor of God.
    - Soul - Seek wisdom. (When, how and if to do what.)
    - Body - Diet, exercise, rest.
- Turn problems into challenges.
- Develop the skill of problem-solving.
- Keep going.

Failing is a temporary setback and is part of the journey. Quitting is throwing in the towel and dropping out of the race. "Whatever is worth doing, is worth doing *badly* rather than not doing it at all." A courageous try based on faith scores higher with God than a good performance based on self-confidence.

Example - Ice Skating for a gold medal. The score is higher for one who performs a difficult choreography and has a fall, than one who skates an easier program flawlessly.

July 26

A SET-BACK

How to deal with a bad, low-score performance -
Proverbs 24:16; Micah 7:8; 2 Corinthians 4:8-11

- Tell yourself that you <u>did </u>try. When you try and fail, you are not a failure.
      You are only a failure when, you don't try at all.
- Analyze the score and learn from your mistakes.
- Gain a proper perspective through the Serenity Prayer.
- Focus on your actions, not on other people or circumstances.
- Confess, repent, forgive and release.
- Prepare for the next challenge.

July 27

IT IS FINISHED !
John 19:30

These were the final words of Jesus at the age of 33 on the Cross at Calvary.
Though there were thousands Jesus did not heal, hundreds of villages He did not visit, multitudes He did not help, He had still completely fulfilled God's plan for His life.

July 28

GOOD FEELINGS

- Mental stability - Serenity, tranquility, calmness, equanimity, peace, dialogue, everything under control and in order.
- Physical well-being – Having eaten the right kind and amount of food. Regular meals, rest and sleep.
- Accomplishments - Having completed a task well.
- Relief - Having received good news, found a lost article or sold something.
- The love and affection of a pet.
- Beauty in nature, music and art.
- Changing weather patterns.
- Good dialogue, humor, situation comics.
- Intimate moments with the Lord.

July 29

BAD FEELINGS

- Being out of tune spiritually, out of harmony mentally and out of step physically with myself, others, nature and God.
- Being under pressure. Having to rush or wait.
- Being surrounded by strife, tension, violence, arguments, noise and chaos.
- Being hungry or overstuffed, tired or hyper. Being dirty and unattractive.
- Discomfort and pain.
- Fear and anxiety.
- Anger and resentment.
- Ridicule and shame.
- Guilt and remorse.
- "If only......"

July 30

TWO LAWS OF NATURE

- *A qualitative law* - You reap what you sow.
- *A quantitative law* - You reap more than you sow.

Reputation is what others <u>think</u> you are.
Character is what God <u>knows</u> you are.

July 31

THE SUFFICIENCY OF GOD

- God loves me unconditionally, therefore I can love myself and others. Jeremiah 31:3
- God forgives me, therefore I can forgive myself and others. Colossians 3:13
- God is sovereign, there are no accidents. Deuteronomy 4:35; Daniel 4:35
- God knows me, therefore I will not be misunderstood. Psalm 139
- God's grace is sufficient for my afflictions. 2 Corinthians 12:9
- God provides for my spiritual, emotional and physical needs. Philippians 4:19
- God is faithful, therefore I can trust Him. Numbers 23:19; Deut 7:9; Lam 3:22-25
- God provides strength, therefore I can endure this trial moment by moment, one day at the time. 1 Corinthians 15:58; Galatians 6:9; Philippians 4:13; 2 Tim 2:3-5

August 1

DON'T MISS OUT

The consequences of living your life apart from God -

- To ignore His Word is to travel without a map.
- To ignore His warnings is to meet disaster and judgment.
- To ignore His promises is to miss out on His blessings.
- To ignore His invitations is to miss out on the love, joy peace and contentment of a personal relationship with God.

August 2

THE TEN P's OF PRAYER

WHAT TO PRAY FOR -

Protection,
        Provision,
                Peace,
                        Purpose,
                                Plan,
                                        Perspective,
                                                Patience,
                                                        Power,
                                                                Perseverance,
                                                                        Performance.

August 3

FROM PAIN TO PEACE

Diagnosis and remedies for emotional pain -

PAIN - Inability to be and do what pleases God. Matthew 26:41; Romans 7:18-19
PEACE - Confess and repent and apply the blood of Christ. 1 John 1:9

PAIN - Being misunderstood by the lack of interest, narrowness or superficiality of
      other people. John 1:10-11; 6:60; 7:5, 8, 43; 21:23
PEACE - Talk it over with Jesus, who understands the problem as no one else can.
      Matthew 11:28-30; Mark 1:35

PAIN - To be with people who deny and complain, but neither seek nor apply solutions
      to their problems. Proverbs 1:7; Jeremiah 32:33; 44:16; Zechariah 7:11;
      Matthew 23:37; Romans 3:11
PEACE - Detach yourself and let them go. Matthew 7:6; 10:14; 1 Corinthians 5:11;
      2 Corinthians 6:14-18; 2 Thessalonians 3:6, 14, 15

PAIN - To be afflicted by the sins of others. Matthew 27:29-31; Hebrews 11:36-38
PEACE - Trust. Deut 31:8; Prov 3:5-6; Isa 26:3; Rom 8:28; 2 Cor 12:9-10
      Obey. Joshua 22:5; 1 Samuel 15:22; Jeremiah 7:23; Romans 6:17;
      Praise. Psalms 34:1; 150; 1 Peter 2:9

August 4

PAST, PRESENT, FUTURE

GAINS and ASSETS from the PAST -
      Experience, understanding, knowledge, wisdom, courage, strength, compassion
      and answered prayers.
      1 Samuel 7:12; 12:24; Psalm 103:1-2

OPPORTUNITIES for TODAY -
      Enthusiasm for the task at hand. (En Theos: in God)
      Psalm 118:24; Ecclesiastes 9:10; Colossians 3:23

HOPE for the FUTURE -
      The best is yet to come. God is in charge, bringing His Kingdom to pass.
      Isaiah 65:17; John 16:33; Revelation 21:1-7

        "Lord, I am willing to receive what you give, to lack what you withhold, to
        relinquish what you take, to suffer what you inflict, to go where you lead,
        to do what you ask and to be what you have created me for."

August 5

WOUND DRESSING

How to neutralize and diffuse irritation, resentment and anger -

- Retreat to a quiet place and talk it over with Jesus. Matthew 11:28-30; Mark 1:35
- Cleanse the wound by confession and repentance. 1 John 1:9
- Apply the disinfectants called forgiveness and intercession. Matthew 5:44-45
- Dress the wound with the soothing balm of thanksgiving and praise. Eph 5:19-20

Take this opportunity to grow and mature spiritually.

August 6

LABELS FOR DIFFERENT WELLS

EMPTY WELLS - Looking for something in other people that they cannot deliver, leads
to frustration, anger and depression. Parents, siblings, spouses, children and friends cannot
possibly meet all your needs. God has placed in all of us a heart-shaped vacuum, that only
He can fill.

POISONED WELLS - Food, drugs, alcohol, tobacco, sex, lotteries, entertainment and
religions can soothe the symptoms of loneliness for a while, but will never deliver the
satisfaction we crave.

HEALTHY WELLS -
God, Jesus Christ, the Holy Spirit for Love, Joy and Peace.
The Bible for Wisdom.
Books, tapes, radio for Knowledge.
Nature, music, pets for Happiness.
Physical exercise for Well-being.
Agenda, work for Satisfaction.

August 7

TO BE HOLY
Leviticus 11:44

HOW	-	Through Jesus Christ.
WHEN	-	Now, in the present.
WHERE	-	Here, where you are.
WITH WHOM	-	The person you are facing right now.

August 8

RESPONSE TO CRITICISM

Steps in the wrong direction:

- Blaming God, others and circumstances - *Wrong focus.*
- Rebuking Satan - *Unconfessed sin gives him legal access into your life.*
- Partial confession - *Denial based on an illusion..*
- Praising God - *He does not want praise or sacrifice when you are in disobedience.*
- Insisting on personal rights - *Sin of pride.*
- Bitterness and revenge - *Sin of unforgiveness.*
- Self-pity - *Sin of ingratitude.*
- Seeking relief through alcohol, drugs, food, sex, material things - *Sin of idolatry.*

Steps in the right direction:

- Confession - *To agree with God.*
- Repentance - *To make a U-turn.*
- Forgiveness - *To ask and accept.*
- Recovery - *To rebuild*
- Acknowledge the sovereignty of God - *He is in control.*
- Trust the justice of God - *He has the last word.*
- Obey the Word - *It contains the wisdom you need.*
- Praise - *To gain the proper perspective.*

August 9

THE LORD'S PRAYER
Matthew 6:9-13

GOD'S PATERNITY	-	We are God's children by adoption through Jesus Christ.
GOD'S PERSON	-	Fear His holiness.
GOD'S PROGRAM	-	Trust His sovereignty.
GOD'S PURPOSE	-	Submit to His will.
GOD'S PROVISION	-	His grace is sufficient for today.
GOD'S PARDON	-	Receive and grant forgiveness.
GOD'S PROTECTION	-	We are safe under His care.

August 10

AN ONGOING QUEST

- Accepting the people I cannot change. Romans 14:4, 10; Eph 4:32; Col 3:12-13
- Willingness to change myself and take responsibility for my own choices. Rom 14:12
- Trust that God will fill all my needs. Psalm 23:1; Philippians 4:19
- Learning contentment. Philippians 4:11; 1 Timothy 6:6-8
- Praise for the way things are. Psalm 118:24; Phil 4:4; 1 Thessalonians 5:18

August 11

IN TANDEM

Two feet are necessary for walking.
>   The right foot takes the first step, the left foot follows.

Mercy - Grace
>   Justification - Sanctification
>   Mind - Will
>   Decision - Action
>   Faith - Work
>   Trust - Obedience
>   Thanksgiving - Petition
>   Listening - Talking
>   Praise - Worship

>   The one exception is <u>LOVE</u> and <u>TRUTH</u>
>   They are both of equal importance.

>   *Love without Truth has no foundation.*
>   *Truth without Love has no heart.*

August 12

THREE BIG WORDS

<u>JUSTIFICATION</u>   -   The securing of a favorable verdict by Christ's death.
>   A clean slate. "Accepted in the Beloved."
<u>SANCTIFICATION</u>   -   The process of growing in Christ-likeness.
>   The spiritual journey through life.
<u>GLORIFICATION</u>   -   End of the boot camp. Graduation from the school of life.
>   The beginning of a new journey through eternity.

August 13

A HEALTHY PLANT

"Holistic Wellness" presents the ideal condition for the development of ourselves from a tiny seed, the individual God-spark, on to conformity to the image of Christ.

- Body - The soil has to be worked by plowing (exercise), fed by nutrients (proper diet) and receive adequate rest (sleep).
- Soul - Water is needed for cleansing, refreshment and growth.
- Spirit - The sun is needed for light, warmth and comfort.

All three, soil, rain and sun, are essential for the seed to develop and the plant to grow.

August 14

TO BE A FRIEND

Seven important guidelines for being a friend.

- Awareness - To be sensitive and discerning.
- Acceptance - To be free of prejudice and criticism.
- Availability - To be there when needed.
- Listening - To give undivided attention.
- Sharing - To relate your own experience with joy and sadness.
- Gentleness - To ask: "How would Jesus deal with this person?"
- Intercession - To stand in the gap by praying.

August 15

WISDOM

Wisdom is the ability to see a situation or a person from God's point of view; to gain a spiritual perspective and respond accordingly. To know what to do with what you know.

The two lobes of the brain -

- Cognizance - Left brain. Masculinity. Leadership, analytical ability, reason.
- Intuition - Right brain. Femininity. Submission, perception, emotional response.

Wisdom is based on the Word of God,
transformed by the love of Christ,
energized by the Holy Spirit.

August 16

FREEDOM OF CHOICE

God's Word provides a road map and instruction for our journey through life.

THREE OPTIONS -

- We can ignore the instructions and keep on traveling.
- We can deliberately take a different way.
- We can obey and follow the instructions.

CONSEQUENCES -

When we sin by following option one or two, we experience guilt. At that point we can

CHOOSE BETWEEN -

Deny or ignore the conviction OR confess the wrong and agree with God.
Rationalize our actions OR repent and change directions.
Become angry and bitter OR receive and give forgiveness.
Blame others and God OR repair our own mistakes.
Indulge in self-pity OR in peace, joy and contentment.
Experience death - Experience new life.

August 17

THE SPIRIT FILLED LIFE

In order for God to make us like His Son, He has to deal with everything in our lives that does not reflect Jesus Christ. We often go to God for advice, but He never gives advice. Advice is something we can accept or reject, but God tells us what to do. His Word contains commands, not suggestions.

The spirit-filled life is not measured how well we perform in front of others. It is a life of reflection - how much of God's Son we truly reflect to those around us. It is also a life of trust that abandons all we hold dear and seek God above all things. When we grasp the depth of His love, we are no longer worried about our performance. All that we are is wrapped up in who He is.

God's Umbrella of Love consists of –

MERCY	-	He does not give us what we deserve.
CHASTISEMENT	-	He prunes the tree, molds the clay, burns the dross, blows away the chaff and separates the wheat from the tares.
GRACE	-	He gives us what we don't deserve.

August 18

EFFECTIVE INTERCESSION

- Since thoughts are able to travel and contact others, we can either bind them to their problems or set them free by clearing the channel for God to intervene.
- As transmitters, we can send God's saving power and creative redemption to the minds of other people.
- Instead of making our own petitions in behalf of others, we can let the Holy Spirit intercede for their true needs.
- All thoughts originate from one of four sources: The world, the flesh, the Devil or God. We have to make sure that we are connected to the right source, because thoughts can be transmitted to others whether we are aware of it or not.
- To pray in Jesus name means that the prayers are initiated, controlled and directed by Him and in complete alignment with His will.
- When we pray for others, we position them in the light so God can bless them.

August 19

PING-PONG GAME

True communication requires the active participation of two people.

- *To serve a ball* -   To initiate a topic.
- *Refusal to play* -   No response.
- *To play absentmindedly* -   To fake it, act as if, to be distracted.
- *To play aggressively* -   To seek an argument.
- *To take the ball and run with it* - To ramble on, go off on tangents.
- *To serve only* -   To engage in a monologue.

August 20

THIS AND THAT

God does not merely want to be an information center for us, but to build a personal, intimate relationship with each individual. God is more interested in revealing <u>Himself</u> than revealing details about His will. Determine to abide in the love of God regardless of the circumstances. Wait for His timing and rest in His sufficiency. Be grateful for yesterday, eager for tomorrow, but live for today.

God's sovereignty is revealed in the order of the universe.
God's holiness is revealed in His Word.
God's love is revealed in Christ.

August 21

HEADING FOR THE PROMISED LAND

CROSSING THE RED SEA -

- Admit that I am a sinner. Romans 3:23
- Acknowledge that Christ died for my sins. Romans 5:8; 6:23
- Accept Christ as personal Savior. John 1:12; 3:3-21, 36

CROSSING THE JORDAN RIVER -

- Self (id, ego, Adamic nature, flesh, inner child, old man) must abdicate the throne
  in the center of my personality to the Lord Jesus Christ. 2 Chronicles 20:12;
  Luke 14:11, 33; John 3:30; Romans 12:1-2; James 4:10
- Self must be crucified. Romans 6:3-13; 2 Corinthians 4:11; Galatians 2:20; 6:14
- Christ is in me, and I am in Him. John 17:23; 2 Corinthians 5:15-17;
  Philippians 3:8-10; Colossians 1:27; 2:10; 3:3-4

LIVING IN THE PROMISED LAND -

A time of personal growth, maturity, battles, defeats, victories, setbacks,
  challenges, progress, tests and endurance contests.
2 Chronicles 20:15, 17; Romans 6:14; 7:15-25; 8:28-39; 2 Corinthians 3:18; 4:10-11;
Philippians 1:6, 21; 2:5, 12-13; 3:10; James 1:2-4; 1 Peter 4:12-13, 19; 1 John 3:2-3;

August 22

HEALING OF DAMAGED EMOTIONS

- Recall your memories.
- Identify the feelings you had originally (mad, sad, glad, scared, pained, ashamed).
- Relive the scene with Jesus at your side.
- Replace broken images with beautiful scenery.
- Erase the painful tapes and record a new song.
- Give thanks for the past.
- Rejoice in today.
- Give praise for the future.

Ask yourself: What is the worst thing that has ever happened to you?
              What is the best thing that has ever happened to you? Finding Jesus.
              Where was Jesus when the worst thing happened?
He was hanging on the cross in utter physical, emotional and spiritual agony to secure
forgiveness and eternal life for all those who turn to Him for redemption.

August 23

HEALING FOR DAMAGED RELATIONSHIPS

- Picture yourself and the person you have a conflict with, alone together in a pleasant surrounding. Think of what that person could say or do to make it easier for you to forgive. Then watch the person come out of denial, opposition or aggression and actually say the words you want to hear.
- Feel your resentment turn into love, joy and peace as the healing transformation unfolds.
- Picture the person you resented surrounded by light, warmth and beauty, smiling and happy.
- Make this vision a true reality for yourself, witnessed, documented and sealed by God Himself, regardless of the other person's present attitude or behavior.

August 24

MY NEEDS - GOD'S PROMISES

- *GOAL* - To journey towards the Kingdom of God. Matthew 6:33
- *TRANSFORMATION* - To be conformed to Christ.
    Romans 8:29; 2 Corinthians 3:18; 5:17; 1 John 3:2-3
- *WORK* - To be a transmitter for God. Ezekiel 22:30
- *CONNECTIONS WITH LIFE* - Being in touch with God, others and self.
    Isaiah 54:2-3; Ephesians 3:16-19
- *QUALITY OF LIFE* - The Fruit of the Spirit.
    Psalm 16:9; Jeremiah 29:11; John 10:10; 15:11; 16:24; Galatians 5:22-23
- *GUIDANCE, COURAGE, STRENGTH* - For life.
    Deuteronomy 31:8; Joshua 1:9; 2 Chronicles 20:12, 15, 17;
    Psalms 16:11; 32:8; Philippians 4:13
- *HEALING FOR FROZEN EMOTIONS* -
    Exodus 15:26; Psalm 147:3; Isaiah 61:3; Jeremiah 17:14
- *UNDERSTANDING and COMPASSION* -
    Psalm 139; Isaiah 65:24; Hebrews 4:15

August 25

THOSE "OTHER" PROMISES

Adversities, sufferings, physical pain, mental agony, losses, disappointments, injustice.

Zechariah 13:9; Matthew 5:11; John 15:20; Acts 14:22; Romans 8:17;
2 Timothy 3:12; James 1:2-3; 1 Peter 2:21

August 26

TWELVE STEPS OUT OF BONDAGE

- Acknowledge that a problem exists and help is needed. Romans 3:23; 1 John 1:8
- Search for a higher power. God is greater than any problem. Jeremiah 29:12-13
- Accept the help that comes through His Word, circumstances and friends.
    Psalm 119:71; Isaiah 30:21; James 5:14
- Write your life's story. Feel the emotions. Hebrews 4:15
- Share it with God and another person. 1 John 1:9; James 5:16
- Neutralize the hurt with the Word. Exodus 15:23-26; Psalms 19:9-10; 119:11
- Honestly evaluate your responsibility and make amends.
    Proverbs 18:17; Matthew 5:23-25
- Forgive and set up boundaries. The past is in the "library" for reference only.
    Matthew 6:14-15; John 8:32; 2 Corinthians 6:17
- Evaluate your options. Make conscious choices.
    Joshua 24:14-15; Kings 18:21; Proverbs 4:23-27
- Monitor daily your spirit, soul and body.
    Proverbs 4:18; Romans 13:14; Ephesians 5:14-17; Philippians 2:15
- Get in touch with your redeemed self, and you will discover God's will for you.
    Psalm 37:4-5; Matthew 7:7
- Help others by setting them free, respecting them, seeing them in the light and
    warmth of love, sharing your ideas, experiences and emotions.
    Matthew 5:14-16, 44; 10:8; Romans 12:10, 15; Philippians 2:3-4;
    1 Peter 1:22; 4:10; Revelation 12:11

August 27

ASPECTS OF LOVE

In the realm of the SPIRIT -
    Pure Agape love flows from God to us and is channeled through us to others.

In the realm of the SOUL -

<u>Mind</u> -	Protection, provision, respect, interest, freedom, concern, compassion, boundaries and detachment when needed.
<u>Will</u> -	Choice, decision, commitment.
<u>Emotions</u> -	Affection, warmth, attachment, desire for closeness, enjoyable togetherness, bliss, infatuation, ecstasy.

In the realm of the BODY -
    Non-sexual caresses and hugs, physical attraction, sexual desire and fulfillment.

August 28

SOURCES OF DEPRESSION

- *SPIRITUAL* - Unconfessed sin, root of bitterness, unforgiveness.
  - *Solution* - Connect with Jesus. Matthew 11:28-30
    - Study the Word. Psalm 119
    - Obey the Holy Spirit. 1 Kings 19:12; Isaiah 30:21

- *EMOTIONAL* - Low self-esteem, frozen feelings, codependency, fear, anger, compulsive behavior.
  - *Solution* - Counseling, analysis of childhood traumas, Twelve Step programs, group therapy. John 8:32; Hebrews 10:24-25; James 5:14

- *PHYSICAL* - Chemical imbalance in the brain, food allergies, toxins in the body, overweight, lack of exercise and rest.
  - *Solution* - Medication. Diet (restrict sugar, fat, refined flour, caffeine, salt, meat, dairy, processed foods). Physical fitness (aerobics, isometrics). Exodus 15:26; 1 Corinthians 3:16-17; James 5:16

- *DEMONIC* - Stronghold and oppression by Satan.
  - *Solution* - Prayer, armor of God, praise, worship, exorcism, fasting. Matthew 17:21; Ephesians 6:11-18; 1 Peter 5:7-9

- *REJECTION of SELF* - Melancholic temperament, desire to be somebody else.
  - *Solution* - Find out who you are. Accept God's design. Confess ungratefulness and envy. Focus on your strength. Rejoice in your uniqueness. Embrace the challenge. Help others to find and accept themselves. Psalm 139:1-4, 13-16

August 29

PRICELESS

Intimacy with God.

Mercy - not getting the punishment I deserve.

Grace - getting the blessings I don't deserve.

Love - in harmony with God, others and self.

Joy - being content and at peace.

Wisdom - right application of knowledge.

August 30

TO PARTAKE

To partake means to share in, become connected to, enmeshed with, take part in, engage in, become attached to and identify with.

- *CHRIST -*   Hebrews 3:14
- *SUFFERING -*   2 Corinthians 1:7; Colossians 1:24; 2 Timothy 1:8; 1 Peter 4:13
- *HEAVENLY CALLING -*   Matthew 20:16; Hebrews 3:1;
- *HOLY SPIRIT -*   Hebrews 6:4
- *INHERITANCE -*   Colossians 1:12; 1 Timothy 6:2
- *DIVINE NATURE -*   2 Peter 1:4
- *HOLINESS -*   Hebrews 12:10
- *GRACE -*   Philippians 1:7
- *GLORY -*   1 Peter 5:1

It is not enough to do our best to be like Christ. To "be like Christ" does not mean to copy His lifestyle or mimic His mannerism, trying to be patient, tolerant, loving and kind. It is not achieved by positive thinking, self-help, hang-in-there, stick-to-it, trying our best by teeth-gritting determination. It is only when we partake of Him, share in His life, read His Word, abide in His presence, converse with Him, seek His counsel, delight in His fellowship and please Him because we love Him.

August 31

THE RACE OF LIFE
Hebrews 12:1-3

- *Lay aside every encumbrance -* anything that holds you back from being all God wants you to be.
- *Run with endurance -* Don't give up. There may be times you wonder if you will ever see the finish line, but you will. God has promised it.
- *Fix your eyes on Jesus -* Many, like Peter, take their eyes off Christ and focus on the shifting wind and high waves of life. But if you will keep your eyes firmly on Jesus, you will not fail, but receive the Crown of Life.

Isaiah 41:13 "I, the Lord your God, will hold your right hand saying to you: Fear not!"

God does not shield us from difficulties,
but takes our hand and leads us through.

September 1

OUR FREE WILL

To create us in His image, God gave us a free will. We are not puppets on a string or hallow mannequins. Yet to give as free will, God had to relinquish the use of force against us. There is no freedom when there is a gun pointed at us. God does not lack the power to punish or destroy us, but in His love for us, He has chosen never to use it. He intervenes only when asked to help, never to hurt.

Having forsworn the use of power and force against us, He has no alternative but to watch with a broken heart when we turn our backs on Him. He chooses not to prevent the atrocities that we commit upon one another. He will offer us a way to Himself, but He cannot make us to abide with Him.

For the time being, God waits for us through one painful hardship after another. And it may seem to us that we are doomed by this strange, impotent and uncaring God. But the vicarious death of Jesus Christ and His resurrection have overcome evil for all times. The Cross connects us spiritually to God, who will never leave us nor forsake us. In our humanity, the body and soul (mind, will, emotions) are still on the battlefield, but our regenerate spirit is the lifeline to God's omniscience, omnipotence and omnipresence.

September 2

DIRECTIONS FROM ABOVE

- We plan wisely, but we know that God's will prevails. Proverbs 16:9
- We work diligently, but under God's direction. Psalm 127:1-2
- We pray earnestly, but knowing that God's response is always best. Jeremiah 33:3
- We cease striving, because we know that He is God. Psalm 46:10
- We don't have to force our way through life, because God is in control.
  2 Chronicles 20:15, 17; 32:7-8
- We don't have to carry a heavy load, because He invites us to cast our burdens
  on Him. Psalm 55:22; 1 Peter 5:7
- We don't have to manipulate circumstances, because our wise God has a good
  and kind plan. Jeremiah 29:11; Romans 8:28
- We don't have to yield to our weaknesses, because He will provide a way out.
  1 Corinthians 10:13; 2 Peter 2:9

Remembering God's help in the past provides *PROOF* of His faithfulness.
Using each day as a new opportunity to please God gives a *PURPOSE*.
Connecting with Jesus assures *PEACE*.

September 3

TAKING CHARGE

Don't wait for an outside event to make you feel OK, you may not have any control over those circumstances. Instead focus on what you <u>can</u> control. You can turn an adverse reaction into a positive response. Take full responsibility for what you are feeling. When you blame someone else for the way you feel, you give them the power to cause an emotional reaction inside of you. But when you take charge over your feelings, the power comes back to you. Then you realize that you have choices. You are no longer a victim of another person or adverse situations.

Consider these alternatives -

I can't - I won't.
        I should - I could.
                It's a problem - It's an opportunity.
                        Life is a struggle - Life is an adventure.
                              I hope - I know.
                                    If only… - Next time.
                                            What will I do? - I can handle it

September 4

LETTING GO

A decision to let go comes from the realization that I can't control another person, certain situations or God. The outcome is not in my hands.

- It is not to enable, but to allow others to learn from natural consequences.
- It is not to fix, but to be supportive
- It is to grant freedom to others.
- It is not to deny reality, but to accept it.
- It is not to regret the past, but to learn and grow from it.

My reaction to a certain adversity can hurt me more than the situation itself.

September 5

THE TWO PARTS OF THE BRAIN

<u>Right side</u> -   Creativity, thoughts, feelings, intuition, emotions, mood, fantasies.
<u>Left side</u> -   Logic, order, discipline, legalism, perfectionism, math, languages.

September 6

A PERSONAL PROFILE

My personal temperament - <u>Melancholic</u>

- *Needs -*   Security, dialogue, harmony, roots.
- *Weaknesses -*   Perfectionism, insecurity, approval seeking, low stress tolerance, fear of sudden accidents.
- *Strengths -*   Dependable, loyal, faithful, responsible, compassionate, good listener.
- *Major interests -* God, Jesus, Holy Spirit, Bible study, different religions, psychology, spiritual, emotional and physical fitness, languages, problem solving, nature, music, horses, environment, nutrition, exercise.
- *Dislikes -*   Assumptions made without knowing the facts, covert actions behind my back, "silent treatments", shouting matches, anger outbursts, compulsive talkers (subject trivia), people who never ask questions, visits while eating, telephone calls, parties, chaos, noise, having to rush or wait, sunny cloudless days.

September 7

A PERSONAL LETTER FROM GOD

Dear Child,

I have brought you to this place in your life in spite of obstacles and detours. You are exactly where I want you to be. You are doing exactly what I want you to do.

Obey me today, trust me for tomorrow and praise me continuously.

I will always love you.

God.

September 8

WHAT HAS TAKEN PLACE

- God created the world and had dominion over it. Genesis 1:1-25; Psalm 24:1
- God gave the dominion over the earth to man. Genesis 1:26-28
- Man transferred the dominion to Satan by yielding to his temptation. Man knowingly disobeyed God's specific command. Genesis 3:1-6
- God sent His Son to rescue man from the grip of Satan. John 3:16
- Christ paid the penalty of sin for us by His death. Ephesians 2:16
- Christ defeats Satan by His resurrection. 1 Peter 1:3-4
- Man can make a conscious choice to follow God or Satan. Satan <u>cannot</u> get into a man's heart without his consent, and God <u>will</u> not. John 3:17-21
- When man voluntarily commits himself to God's plan of salvation and connects to His power by prayer, Satan will have to retreat - angrily, reluctantly, slowly, stubbornly contesting every inch of the way. James 4:7; 1 John 4:4

September 9

TRUTH ONCE DESPISED
Mark 7:32-33; 8:22-25

In order to heal these men, Jesus spat on them - a most repulsive and humiliating act.
Likewise we will be blessed by the very words, people, circumstances, pains, losses and hardships we once despised. It will make no more sense to us now than trees walking around. But if God has touched your life once, He will touch it again. Philippians 1:6

September 10

HOW GOD ANSWERS PRAYERS

- When conditions are not right, He says: *"NO".*

- When the time is not right, He says: *"SLOW".*

- When we are not right, He says: *"GROW".*

- When everything is right, He says: *"GO".*

September 11

WHEN CALAMITY STRIKES

The world around you is shattered, your heart is broken, your mind is numb, your will is paralyzed, your emotions are raging out of control. Trusting God, focusing on Jesus and hoping for Heaven, are no longer even an option. Praying becomes an exercise in futility.

That is when the Holy Spirit, the Comforter, takes over. Living on the inside of you, He witnesses your turmoil, understands your fear and feels your pain. John 14:16-18. No words are necessary to reach the Throne of God. Romans 8:26-27. Jesus is at the right hand of God, relaying the messages to Him. Romans 8:34; Hebrews 7:25; 9:24. God always hears Jesus. John 11:41-42. (The only time God did not answer Jesus' plea was on the cross, when Jesus took the sins of the whole world upon Himself, and the Father could no longer communicate with His Son). Matthew 27:46

When we have completely surrendered our spirit, soul, body and everything that pertains to our personal life, as well as all the forces beyond our control, we no longer have to struggle with what, how and when to pray.   *Our very life itself has become a prayer.*

September 12

THE FURNACE OF AFFLICTION
Isaiah 48:10

When things go haywire or are not moving at all, our first impulse is to do something to remedy, rectify or resolve the problem. Could not our enemies, disappointments, threats, injustice and uncertainties be better defeated by rolling up our sleeves, making a fist and meeting them head-on? No. We learn from Jehoshaphat that praise must be our first line of defense. 2 Chronicles 20:21

Let's offer sincere, wholehearted praise to God as we walk through the refiner's fire. Perhaps those who pause to peer into our furnace, will see the Son of Man walking with us. Daniel 3:24-27

September 13

RECYCLING

God can recycle past sins, wrong decisions and broken dreams into steppingstones to a life on a higher plane, for a closer walk with Him.

He can also take our physical, emotional and mental illnesses, acute and chronic pain and economic hardships and use them as rungs on the ladder to Heaven.

September 14

THE GOSPEL OF JOHN

THE PERSON - John, the disciple Jesus loved. John 19:26; 21:7

THE PURPOSE - To prove that Jesus is the Son of God. John 1:1-3

THE PROMISE - To assure that all who believe in Christ will have eternal life.
John 3:16; 20:31

Did you know that God has a need only <u>you</u> can fill?
That is why He has created you just the way you are.

September 15

WHAT LIES AHEAD

In the life to come, the grace of God allows us to share in the glory of Christ –

- A love that cannot be imagined.
- A life that cannot end.
- A righteousness that cannot be tarnished.
- A peace that cannot be explained.
- A rest that cannot be disturbed.
- A joy that cannot be diminished.
- A hope that cannot be disappointed.
- A message that cannot be misunderstood.
- A connection that cannot be broken.
- A strength that cannot be weakened.
- A purity that cannot be defiled.
- A beauty that cannot be marred.
- A light that cannot be extinguished
- A wealth that cannot be exhausted.
- A trust that cannot be betrayed.

ONLY ETERNITY IS LONG ENOUGH FOR GOD TO SHARE HIS LOVE WITH US

September 16

THE A B C OF LOVE

A	Accepts others as they are.
B	Believes in their potentials.
C	Cares about the lives and interests of others.
D	Desires the very best for others.
E	Edifies and encourages others.
F	Forgives freely and unconditionally.
G	Gives generously of self, time and possessions.
H	Honors the unique worth of others.
I	Intercedes for others.
J	Jettisons criticism, gossip and worries.
K	Keeps promises and commitments.
L	Loosens expectations and control.
M	Mends broken relationships.
N	Nurtures the needs of others.
O	Overcomes irritations.
P	Perseveres in adversities.
Q	Questions if my words are true, kind and necessary.
R	Reaches out to others.
S	Shares the happiness and sorrows of others.
T	Transmits spiritual blessings.
U	Understands the different perspectives of others.
V	Validates the feelings of others.
W	Warns others about the dangers of the world, the flesh and the devil.
X	X-rays my own motives in dealing with others.
Y	Yields my own rights to others.
Z	Zeroes in on the good and positive traits of others.

September 17

PRAYER FOR OTHERS

CONVICTION - John 16:8

CONFESSION - Romans 10:10

CONVERSION - John 3:16, 36

COMPREHENSION - Colossians 1:9

COMMITMENT - Psalm 37:5

COVER - Psalm 91:4

COMFORT - John 14:16-18

September 18

NON-NEGOTIABLE TRUTHS

- His deity.
- His humanity.
- His virgin birth.
- His perfect life.
- His atoning death.
- His bodily resurrection.
- His personal return.

Jesus is coming back. We don't know when. We should be ready to meet Him anytime.

September 19

ELECTION AND FREE WILL

Both are true and taught in the Bible. You stand before a door over which is written :
"Whosoever will may come." John 3:16; Romans 10:13

As you step by faith through that door, you look back and see the words written :
"Chosen before the foundation of the world." Ephesians 1:4; 1 Peter 1:2

But three times the Lord speaks these terrifying words: "Depart from me." They announce the doom of the disobedient. These individuals find their lot in the fires of eternal separation from God. This is the ultimate punishment for rejecting Jesus Christ. This is the end of a road paved by a lifetime of choices that left God out. Every decision to go it alone is a choice to embrace the final verdict of the Savior.

Hell is God's great compliment to the reality of human freedom and
the dignity of human choice.

Four ways to die in your sins –

- Be self-righteous. Reject God's remedy for sin.
- Be worldly. Follow the world system.
- Be unbelieving. Create your own belief system.
- Be willfully ignorant. Refuse to read the Bible.

September 20

WHAT IS NEEDED FOR PRAYER

- Time set apart.
    Daniel 6:10; Mark 1:35; Acts 10:9
- A quiet place.
    Matthew 6:6; Luke 5:16
- Confession.
    Psalm 66:18; John 9:31
- Jesus as a Mediator.
    John 14:6; 1 Timothy 2:5; Hebrews 12:24
- The Bible as a textbook.
    Psalm 119; Proverbs 6:23; Matthew 24:35; 2 Timothy 3:16
- The Holy Spirit as a teacher.
    Isaiah 30:21; John 14:26
- Faith as an activator.
    2 Corinthians 5:7; Ephesians 3:12; Hebrews 11:6

September 21

FOUR PILLARS OF CHRISTIANITY

CHRISTMAS - The birth of Christ, when God became man.

GOOD FRIDAY - The crucifixion of Jesus, when sin's penalty was paid.

EASTER - The resurrection of Christ, when the power of death was broken.

PENTECOST - The release of the Holy Spirit as a teacher, intercessor and helper.

September 22

OUR EXAMPLE

Jesus did not come to take us "out of this world", but to give us victory <u>in</u> this world.
The doubt and fear that maybe Christ is not victorious in our situation will cause us to sink. People will say: "She is sinking like I am. Why should I follow her God?"

If we don't practice what we profess, live what we preach, walk what we talk, people won't understand why Jesus came and what Jesus is all about.

The greatest achievement in life is to hear God say: "You have been faithful and done well as my servant. Come and enter into the joy of the Lord."   Matthew 25:21

September 23

EMOTIONS

SADNESS - Feeling unloved, lonely, helpless, hopeless, overlooked, misunderstood, depressed, hurt, unworthy, gloomy, dismal, ashamed, remorseful, blue.

FEAR - Feeling uneasy, insecure, inadequate, confused, shy, intimidated, self-conscious, foolish, apprehensive, alarmed, worried, anxious, terrified, panicked.

ANGER - Feeling annoyed, impatient, frustrated, cranky, aggravated, resentful, offended, hostile, bitter, outraged, mean, furious, spiteful, hateful.

GLADNESS - Feeling accepted, loved, joyful, peaceful, grateful, content, free, refreshed, happy, wonderful, energetic, delighted, warm, cheerful.

Watching the sun set in the <u>WEST</u>, where the Lord has extinguished all our *sadness.*

Weathering the chilling arctic air of *fear* from the <u>NORTH.</u>

Wrestling the blistering heat of *anger* from the <u>SOUTH.</u>

Walking <u>EAST</u> towards the sunrise, the coming of our Lord, with *gladness* in our hearts.

<u>We can keep going under the protection of God's everlasting love.</u>

September 24

HUNGER

God has created in all of us a hunger for spiritual, emotional and physical closeness, but He gave <u>us</u> the freedom to choose how to fill that hunger.

We can turn to religion or idolatry for spiritual needs, to relationships or status for psychological needs and to junk food or fornication for physical needs.

Through the Holy Spirit, God can fill that hunger by transforming us, so we can be connected to God by Communion, to others by compassion and to ourselves by contentment within.

We will gain –
      Greater wisdom and a better perspective.
         Inner peace with more contentment.
            Deeper love, the investment with the greatest dividend.

FOOD FOR THE SOUL
John 6:48-58

The things we think about are the things we feed on. As Christians, our thoughts should not just be about Christ but they must reflect what Christ would think if He were in our circumstances. This is what it means to feed on Him and be nourished by the Bread of Life.

If you know Christ and walk in the joy of His presence every day, God will bless you and turn you into someone who reflects Christ. Suffering and success go together. If you are succeeding without suffering, it is because others before you have suffered. If you are suffering without succeeding, it is that others after you may succeed.

We cannot always control or change our circumstances, but we can always choose our attitude in facing them. God does not want promises from us to do better at producing the Fruit of the Spirit. He wants our dependence on Him and a willingness to follow Him wherever He leads. It is the Holy Spirit that brings forth the Fruit in us, if we trust, obey and praise. Then we truly have a harvest to feed on.

DART-BOARD or PIPELINE

Don't let life happen to you, let life happen through you. Change from being a dart-board to becoming a pipeline. As a worn-out dart-board, you are using all your energy to shield yourself from the darts of life's trials. Instead of dodging these fiery missiles, let God's wisdom, love and strength be channeled through you on it's way to help others. Delegate the attacks from the outside to the Cross. There, the sovereignty of God will transform them to comfort, instruct and heal all that are discouraged and down-trodden.

Others will never see the Lord Jesus in us, if the purpose of our lives is self-expression. But if our focus is Christ-expression, then the Holy Spirit will enable others to see Jesus in us.

TO BLESS OTHERS

To transmit God's love.
  To treat them with respect, forgiveness, patience, understanding and kindness.

HELP FROM THE WORD

- *DISCOURAGEMENT* -
    Galatians 6:9 "Do not become weary in doing good, for in due time you will reap
        a harvest."
    Romans 8:18 "The suffering of this present time does not compare to the future
        glory that awaits us."
    2 Corinthians 4:16-18 "The spirit will grow and mature. The temporary affliction
        will bring a reward (increased ability to love and serve God). The
        spiritual reality will be eternal."

- *WORRY* -
    Isaiah 41:10 "Fear not, for I am with you. Be not dismayed, for I am your God."
    Psalm 55:22 "Cast your burdens on the Lord, He will not disappoint you."

- *IRRITATION* -
    Colossians 3:12-13 "By an act of the will, show mercy, kindness, meekness,
        patience and forgiveness."
    Romans 14:10 "Why do you show contempt for your brother? We will all stand
        before the Judgment Seat of Christ."

- *LAZINESS* -
    Colossians 3:17 "Whatever you do, offer your work to Jesus with thanksgiving."

- *GLUTTONY* -
    Proverbs 25:16 "Never eat more than you need. Too much will make you sick."

September 28

FAIR EXCHANGE

All the tomorrows of our lives have to pass by God before they get to us. He will not permit any troubles to come upon us, unless He has a specific plan by which great blessings can come out of the difficulties.

When God tests you, it is a good time for you to test Him. Gather the promises from His Word and pray them back to God. Then you can claim from Him just as much as your trials have rendered necessary.

Luke 12:32 "Fear not, for it is your Father's good pleasure to give you the Kingdom."
Phil 4:19 "God shall supply all your needs according to His riches through Christ Jesus."
Matthew 28:20 "I will be with you always, to the end of this age."

September 29

BROADER PERSPECTIVE

Many of our troubles are caused by self-centeredness. The human mind is not meant to be limited to such a narrow scope. It is to be free to soar, to dream, to hope and to trust. When our eyes are turned inward instead of upward, we suffer from spiritual near-sightedness.

Worry is an old man bent over, carrying a bag of feathers, thinking it is a load of lead.

Real maturity is recognizing that God is all you need to make life worthwhile.

When affliction, pain, trouble and heartache come into your life, seize the opportunity to witness to those around you the love, joy and peace of Christ's presence within you.

There are just as many stars in the sky at noon as at midnight, although we cannot see them in the sun's glare. We will not fully understand our trials and adversities until we are in heaven. Then we will discover how God took care of us and blessed us even in the storms of life. We face dangers every day and not even be aware of. There are angels in heaven whose mission it is to minister to us. Nothing will happen to a child of God by chance.

GOD RULES WITH PERFECT LOVE, INFINITE WISDOM AND ABSOLUTE CONTROL.

September 30

FLAWS

The problems of the disciples and how Jesus dealt with them.

- Lack of understanding spiritual truths. Jesus keeps on teaching.
- Lack of faith. Jesus performs miracles.
- Lack of humility. Jesus lives by example.
- Lack of courage, commitment. Jesus prays and intercedes.
- Lack of power. Jesus sends the Holy Spirit.

Dealing with people is difficult and frustrating. Being without them is lonely.

Forgiveness is not an occasional act. It is a permanent attitude.

You agree to forgive a debt, therefore you agree that it will cost you something.

Agape love is not a feeling, but a decision. It is not a formula, but a Person.

A JOURNEY THROUGH LIFE

THE SHEPHERD - He is with me even though I don't see Him or sense His presence.
Deuteronomy 31:8; Matthew 28:20

THE PATH OF OBEDIENCE - After many detours, it will lead to the High Places.
Joshua 22:5; Psalm 16:7-11; Isaiah 42:16; Habakkuk 3:18-19

NEW NAME - PJC. Peace : In tune with God, others and self.
Joy : Wellbeing of spirit, soul and body.
Contentment : God is in control, all is well.
Isaiah 56:5; 62:1-2; 2 Corinthians 5:17; Revelation 2:17

HANDICAPS - Frozen emotions, physical discomfort.
Isaiah 30:20; John 16:33; 2 Corinthians 12:7-10

COMPANIONS - Frustrations, conflict, disappointments, discouragement.
Romans 12:10-21; Galatians 6:9

OFFERINGS ON THE ALTAR - Expectations, recognition, rights, security.
Mark 8:34; Luke 14:33; 18:28-30

OFFERINGS OF THANKSGIVING - Music, songs, melodies.
2 Kings 3:15; Psalms 33:1-3; 150; Ephesians 5:19

PRAYER ALONG THE WAY - Mercy. Lamentations 3:23. Grace. 2 Corinthians 12:9
Truth. John 8:32. Guidance. Psalm 32:8
Courage. Joshua 1:9. Strength. Isaiah 40:31
Calm the clamor. Psalm 46:10. Clean the clutter. Hebrews 12:1. Close contact. Psalm 27:4.
Construct a channel. Ezekiel 22:30. Clear communication. Isaiah 30:21

DESTINATION - The Kingdom of Love.

To discern the will of God. Matthew 7:7
To please God. 1 Thessalonians 4:1
To be conformed to Christ. Romans 8:29
To learn to love. John 13:35
To serve others. Matthew 20:26-28
To praise and worship God. Revelation 7:11-12

TESTS ALONG THE WAY

ABSENT SHEPHERD -

        Reaction - Feeling abandoned.

        Response - Pray, meditate, listen. Jeremiah 29:12-13; Matthew 28:20

FOG -

        Reaction - Doubts about the right way.

        Response - Proceed by faith. 2 Corinthians 5:7; Hebrews 11:1

STORMS -

        Reaction - Anxiety.

        Response - Focus on peace. Isaiah 26:3

DESERT -

        Reaction - Boredom.

        Response - Explore creativity. Genesis 1:26

HIGH WINDS AND SEAS -

        Reaction - Stress.

        Response - Relax and unwind. Mark 6:31

OBSTACLES -

        Reaction - Frustration.

        Response - Welcome the challenges. Phiippians 4:13; 1 John 4:4

ISOLATION -

        Reaction - Loneliness.

        Response - Solitude. Mark 1:35

DETOURS -

        Reaction - Discouragement.

        Response - Persevere. 1 Corinthians 15:58; Galatians 6:9

UNCERTAINTY -

        Reaction - Worry.

        Response - Trust. Proverbs 3:5-6; Jeremiah 29:11

DANGERS -

        Reaction - Fear.

        Response - Seek shelter. Psalms 46:1; 91:1-16; Isaiah 41:10

TEMPTATIONS -

        Reaction - Struggle.

        Response - Develop a strategy. Rom 13:14; 2 Timothy 2:22; 1 Peter 5:8-9

CRITICISM -

        Reaction - Feeling hurt.

        Response - Evaluate the charges. 1 Corinthians 11:31-32; 2 Cor 13:5-9

SORROW -

        Reaction - Despair.

        Response - Sadness. Psalm 30:5; Luke 19:41-42; John 11:35

HUMILIATION -

        Reaction - Toxic shame.

        Response - Change what you can, accept what you can't, move on.

                James 4:10; 2 Corinthians 12:8-9; Philippians 3:13

SINS
Poisons – Toxins – Germs – Viruses - Tumors

UNBELIEF -

Study the Word. Matthew 22:29; Luke 16:29-31; Romans 15:4

IDOLATRY -

Focus on the Trinity.

God - Sovereignty. Deuteronomy 4:39; Isaiah 45:5-7

Holiness. Psalm 99;9; Revelation 15:4

Love. Jeremiah 31:3; Ephesians 2:4-6

Christ - Sinbearer. 2 Corinthians 5:21

Advocate. Hebrews 7:25; 1 John 2:1

Friend. Proverbs 17:17; John 15:15

Holy Spirit - Teacher. John 14:26; 16:13

Supplier of strength. 1 John 4:4

Helper. Psalm 138:7-8; Romans 8:26; Philippians 1:6

INGRATITUDE -

Give thanks for blessings and adversities.

Genesis 28:47-48; Psalm 34:1; Ephesians 5:20; 1 Thessalonians 5:18

DISHONESTY -

Confess lies immediately. Zechariah 8:16-17; Ephesians 4:25; 1 John 1:9

BITTERNESS -

Forgive others, God and self. Matthew 6:14-15; Romans 12:17-21

PRIDE -

Remember who you are. Proverbs 16:5; Isaiah 64:6; Jer 49:16; James 4:14

SELFISHNESS -

Convert it to self-esteem. Galatins2:20; Colossians 2:9-10

SELF-PITY -

Convert it to compassion for others. Romans 12:15; 2 Cor 1:4; Hebr 13:3

CO-DEPENDENCY -

Create proper boundaries. 2 Corinthians 6:17

GLUTTONY -

Avoid temptation. Proverbs 25:16; Romans 13:14

TOUCHINESS -

Compare your trials with those of Jesus. Hebrews12:1-3; 1 Peter 4:19

IMPATIENCE -

Rely on God's timing. Psalm 90:4; Isaiah 55:8-9; 2 Peter 3:8

PERFECTIONISM -

Learn flexibility. Proverbs 16:9; James 4:13-17

WASTING TIME -

Make an agenda. Proverbs 4:26; Matthew 5:16; Ephesians 5:14-16

ENVIE -

Rejoice with others. Jonah 4:1-11; Matthew 20:1-15; Luke 15:27-32

October 4

MARRIAGE CONTRACT

To honor the commitment to each other for better or for worse.

- Respect each other's individuality. Tolerance for behavior that does <u>not</u> hurt or disrupt others. Examples - hobbies, likes, dislikes, sleeping patterns, schedules, eating preferences.
- Agree that all events in the past have been settled and forgiven. They can be referred to only as impersonal case studies, never used for accusations.
- Commit to be good listening partners and give honest feedbacks. No denials, silent treatments or cover-ups.
- Give each other freedom to share all emotions as they arise, from great joy to deep depression, from affection to anger, from convictions to doubts. No stuffing or hiding feelings.

October 5

RESPONSE TO GOD'S WILL

The will of God for ourselves is like a melody being played. It is up to us to follow, complement and enhance the music. It is an invitation to respond to God's leading with a free spirit and a joyous heart. We are never meant to be in a straight jacket laboring under the heavy hand of a dictator.

PITCH - The spirit must be tuned daily to God's standard by confession, repentance and newness of life. His perfect pitch never changes.
Psalm 119:89; Hebrews 13:8; James 1:17

HARMONY - The soul then is free to respond with chords in harmony to the mode (the setting and framework), the key (the course of action and events) and the melody (God's personal will for us). This is done by discernment and praise. When the melody is difficult and hard to understand, the mind must engage in prayer for guidance, the will must search for the right chords and the emotions must exercise patience.
Unbelief, rebellion and ungratefulness bring forth dissonance and discord.
Psalms 33:3; 150

RHYTHM - The body must be in step with God's timetable.
Ecclesiastes 3:1-9; 2 Peter 3:8

October 6

THE 10 COMMANDMENTS APPLIED
A marriage contract based on the Ten Commandments.

- *LOYALTY* - Don't betray. Exodus 20:3
- *FAITHFULNESS* - Don't look for substitutes. Exodus 20:4-6
- *REVERENCE* - Hold each other in high esteem. Don't malign or gossip. Exodus 20:7
- *INTIMACY* - Take time to be alone with the one you love. Exodus 20:8-11
- *RESPECT* - Submit yourself to the chain of command. Exodus 20:12
- *GENTLENESS* - Do not inflict any hurts. Exodus 20:13
- *PURITY* - Do not defile your union. Exodus 20:14
- *HONESTY* - Don't do anything in secret. Exodus 20:15
- *TRUTHFULNESS* - Be straight forward. Do not lie. Exodus 20:16
- *UNSELFISHNESS* - Be content with what you have. Exodus 20:17

October 7

PRAYER TIPS

Pray : *"According to Your will,"* not *"If it is your will."* The word if gives you an escape
      and an apologetic excuse for God. Make a mental picture of the prayer as
      answered. Leave the *"how"* and *"when"* to God.
When praying for others: Picture the person in the presence of Jesus.
                         See the darkness, fog and clutter disappear.
                         Pray for sensitivity to the Holy Spirit.
                         Pray for God's protection from evil.

October 8

TWO FOUNDATIONS
Matthew 7:24-27

ROCK - Right doctrine. Galatians 1:8-9; Acts 4:12
                  Obedience. John 14:15
                        Pure motive. Psalm 139:23-24

SAND - Error. Proverbs 16:25
                  Self-righteousness. Isaiah 64:6-7
                      Wrong motive. James 4:3

October 9

TO FIND GOD'S WILL

- Pray for guidance. James 1:5
- Evaluate the thoughts that come to your mind. They must be in agreement with Scripture. Psalm 66:18; 139:23-24; Proverbs 28:9; John 9:31; James 4:3
- Act in whatever way is necessary to get the ball rolling. 1 Kings 17:11-16
- Desire only the will of God. Psalms 37:4; 40:8
- Don't get intimidated by the seemingly impossible circumstances. 2 Kings 6:16-17
- Wait for God's timing. Psalm 27:14; 37:7
- Be flexible to accept either fast action or a long wait. Genesis 19:22; 15:2-5
- Live in a atmosphere of praise (Ephesians 5:20), expectation (James 1:6-7), peace (Isaiah 26:3), contentment (Philippians 4:11)

October 10

SOME THOUGHTS

Better than counting your years, make all your years count.

People may doubt what you say, but they believe what you do.

Don't be afraid to trust an unknown future to an all-knowing God.

True humility is not looking down on yourself, but looking up to Christ.

Contentment is not found in having everything, but being satisfied with what we have.

Each hidden sin is a time bomb ticking away, waiting to go off. Confession, repentance and forgiveness are the only way to defuse them.

In order to interest others in becoming Christians, our lives much give them visible evidence that we have more love, joy, peace, patience, gentleness, goodness, faith, meekness and self-control than a moral, respected and upright non-believer.

The world says: The way to find peace is to get all your circumstances under control.
The Word says: The way to find peace is to let the Lord Jesus Christ live in us and transform all circumstances, good and bad, into a blessing for us and glory for Him.

Neurotics are people who build castles in the air, psychotics are those who move into them, and psychiatrists are the ones who collect the rent.

October 11

WHAT IS IDOLATRY ?
Exodus 20:3

- <u>To worship the true God in the wrong way.</u> Isaiah 1:11-15

    Fundamentalists - Emphasis on Truth, but neglecting the Spirit. 2 Corinthians 3:6
    Charismatics - Emphasis on the Spirit, but neglecting the Truth. Matthew 7:21-23
    Catholics - Distortion of the Truth. Romans 3:28; Galatians 1:8-9; 2:16, 21; 3:11;
                Ephesians 2:8-9; 1 Timothy 2:5
                Traditions instead of the Word. Colossians 2:8; Revelation 22:18
    Jews - Incomplete Truth. John 14:6; Acts 4:12; Romans 10:9-10
            Rejection of the Spirit. Romans 8:9

- <u>To create a false image of the true God.</u> Exodus 20:3-4; Romans 1:21-25

    Powerless - resulting in fear and worry.
    Capricious - resulting in insecurity.
    Distant - resulting in self-reliance and ungratefulness.
    Mean-spirited - resulting in intimidation.
    No authority - resulting in disobedience.

- <u>To worship a false god.</u> Exodus 34:14; Judges 2:11-13; 10:6; Jeremiah 44:4-6, 15-30

    Eastern religions.
    All cults.

- <u>To worship the gods of this world.</u> Isaiah 31:1; Jer 17:5; Matthew 6:24; Phil 3:18-19

    Self - Psalm 10:4
    Money - 1 Timothy 6:10
    Fame - Matthew 23:6-7; Mark 9:35; Philippians 2:3-4
    Success - Ecclesiastes 2:10-11
    Power - Daniel 4:25, 30-31; John 19:11
    Material clutter - Matthew 19:21-22; Luke 12;16-21
    Food, alcohol, drugs - Prov 20:1; 23:21; Eccl 6:7; Isaiah 5:11; 28:7; Rom 14:17
    Knowledge - Romans 1:21-22; 1 Corinthians 3:19; 2 Timothy 3:7
    Beauty - 1 Samuel 16:7
    Sex - 1 Corinthians 6:9-10, 18-20; 1 Thessalonians 4:3-4; 2 Timothy 2:22

- <u>To worship Satan.</u> Revelation 13:4

    The result is total depravity, corruption, cruelty, wickedness.
    Genesis 6:5; 1 Samuel 15:23; Proverbs 6:16-19; Jeremiah 17:9

October 12

TO COMMUNICATE WITH GOD

PRAYER - Intimate dialogue with God. Jeremiah 33:3; Psalm 91:15

SUPPLICATION - A humble, urgent request, entreaty, petition, appeal, plea.
Daniel 6:10-11; Philippians 4:6; Hebrews 5:7-8

INTERCESSION - Vicarious prayers for others, to stand in the gap for someone, to
become involved by empathy and compassion.
Ezekiel 22:30; 1 Timothy 2:1

PRAISE - The highest form of communication with God. An unconditional outpouring of
love and gratitude. Psalms 22:3; 100; Habakkuk 3:17-18

October 13

WHAT DOES GOD WANT ?

We often say that we would like to do the will of God, if we would only know what that will is. There are six unmistakable commands in the Bible. Each one leads to more understanding of God's will for our lives. Search the Scriptures.

- Be saved. Matthew 18:14; John 6:40; 2 Peter 3:9
- Be Spirit-filled. Romans 8:9; Ephesians 5:18
- Be sanctified. Romans 12:1-2; 2 Corinthians 6:17; 1 Thessalonians 4:3-4
- Be submissive. Ephesians 5:22-24; 6:6-7; James 4:6-7
- Be willing to suffer. 2 Corinthians 1:3-10; Philippians 1:29; Colossians 1:24;
2 Timothy 3:12; 1 Peter 2:19-24; 3:17; 4:19
- Be thankful. 1 Thessalonians 5:18

Where is the "far country" of the Prodigal son? Anywhere you choose to live outside the will of God. He lovingly targets an area in which we are not submissive, arranges the circumstances, chooses the tools, controls the pressure and the timing to bring us back under His protective care. The more mature we become as Christians, the more dependent we become on God.

What is God's ultimate intention to redeem us? To save us from the lake of fire? To make us servants? To have someone to praise Him? To demonstrate the magnitude of His grace?
No! The supreme reason for creating and saving us is to assure for Himself and us the
inexplicable joy of mutual love throughout eternity.

Jeremiah 31:3; 1 Corinthians 13:13

October 14

HOW SATAN BLINDS PEOPLE

- By undermining the inerrancy and integrity of Scripture. This way he removes the basic foundation and infrastructure of Christianity.
  Deuteronomy 4:2; Ps 119:89; Isaiah 40:8; Matt 24:35; 2 Tim 3:16-17; 1 Pet 1:25
- By exalting self. "I am OK, you are OK." No need for a Savior.
  Isaiah 64:6; Romans 3:23
- By enticing people to create a god that suits their lifestyles.
  Malachi 3:6; Romans 1:21-23; 1 Timothy 2:5; 1 John 3:6-10
- By establishing ethics according to various situations. "When it feels good, do it."
  Proverbs 12:15; 14:12; Isaiah 5:20-21, 24
- By proclaiming other ways to God without Christ.
  John 3:18, 36; 14:6; 1 John 2:23; 4:15
- By considering the Cross foolishness.
  Romans 10:9-10; 1 Corinthians 1:18; 2:14; Galatians 2:21

October 15

MEDITATION DEFINED

Meditation is the act of calling to mind, thinking over, dwelling on and applying to oneself the various ways about the works, purposes and promises of God. It is the activity of a pure mind, consciously performed in the presence of God, under the eye of God, by the help of God and as a means of communion with God.

It's purpose is to clear one's mental and spiritual vision of God and to let His truth make it's full and proper impact on one's mind and heart. It is a matter of talking to oneself about God and talking to God about oneself. It is a way to replace moods, doubts and problems with forgiveness, assurance and grace.

I know that I am accepted by the Father, because He made me.
I know that I am accepted by the Son, because He saved me.
I know that I am accepted by the Holy Spirit, because He indwells me.

When lying awake at night -

> Thank God for each blessing you have received during the day.
> Pray for all the people that enter your mind.
> Picture what Paradise means to you.
> Memorize Bible verses.

October 16

FOUR BASIC PETITIONS

Pray daily for -

- *MERCY* - That God won't give me what I deserve.
    Psalms 103:17; 136:1-26; Lamentations 3:22-23

- *GRACE* - That God gives me what I don't deserve.
    2 Corinthians 12:9; Ephesians 1:6; 2:8-9

- *INSTRUCTION* - That God reveals His will for me.
    Psalms 119:27, 73, 125; 143:8, 10; Proverbs 3:5-6

- *ASSURANCE* - That God's presence helps me every step of the way.
    Deuteronomy 31:6; Psalm 23; Isaiah 40:31; 1 John 4:4

October 17

WHAT GOES WRONG
Why do I fail when I try so hard?

Incomplete dealings with sin.
    Confession - An intellectual agreement with God regarding sin and it's remedy.
        Pharao. Exodus 9:27
        Balaam. Numbers 22:34
        Judas. Matthew 27:3-5
    Repentance - A personal conviction followed by genuine sorrow.
        David. Psalm 51:10-17
        Peter. Matthew 26:75

Incomplete understanding of -
    The power of the Holy Spirit. Romans 7:24-25
    My position in Christ. Romans 6:4-8
    God's method and timing. Isaiah 55:8-9; Philippians 4:19

Incomplete forgiveness of others.
    Matthew 7:1-5; 18:18; Romans 2:1-3; 1 Corinthians 4:5

As pain and fever are indications that something is wrong in our bodies, guilt and lack of joy indicate a spiritual disease.
Don't get rid of the symptoms - look for the causes and eliminate them.

October 18

PROMISES FOR OVERCOMERS

- *Tree of life* - To live in Paradise. Revelation 2:7
- *Eternal life* - Unending bliss. Revelation 21:4-7
- *Hidden Manna* - To be in the presence of Jesus for spiritual food. Revelation 2:17
- *White stone* - Perfect knowledge of God's will. Revelation 2:17
- *New name* - Unique individuality. Revelation 2:17
- *Power over the nations* - Dominion over creation. Revelation 2:26
- *Morning Star* - Christ will live in our hearts. Revelation 2:28
- *White raiment* - Righteousness, purity, holiness. Revelation 3:5
- *Confessed before God* - Accepted in heaven. Revelation 3:5
- *Pillar in the temple* - Being part of the structure of heaven. Revelation 3:12
- *Named after God* - Mark of ownership and legal citizenship. Revelation 3:12
- *Seat on the throne of God* - Place of honor. Revelation 3:21

October 19

GREAT FAITH

Sometimes God does not act in the way we expect Him to. Matthew 15:21-28
The Canaanite woman accepted the rebuke of Jesus and worshipped Him. Then she asked Him to help her with her own need. She took the rejection and drew closer to the Lord. She countered His negative reply with a positive affirmation instead of turning away in bitterness and self-pity.

When things get tangled in a knot and the vision is clouded in a fog, go back to Calvary and spend time at the foot of the Cross. It is OK to cry over shattered dreams. When things are too painful, cuddle up close to the God of all Comfort.

Rigid Bible study can cause you to lose your joy of salvation. Remember that you are a Pearl of great price. You are so precious and loved, that you don't have to depend on the love of others. All hurts are for our good eventually. They teach us how to have compassion for others. They can show the world and the devil how to bring glory to God.
Don't waste any of the hurts!!

Our great reward will be to hear Jesus proclaim :

"O woman, great is your faith!"

October 20

WE CAN BE SURE

SECULAR HOPE - Optimistic outlook that things will turn out OK.

SPIRITUAL HOPE - Desire with the assurance of fulfillment.

- Certainty of the forgiveness of our sins. Psalm 103:12; 1 John 1:9
- Certainty of eternal life. Titus 1:2
- Certainty of God's presence. Matthew 28:20; Hebrews 13:5
- Certainty of God's help in trouble. Psalm 46:1
- Certainty of the fulfillment of our needs. Psalm 145:19; Philippians 4:19
- Certainty of the accomplishment of God's purposes. Isaiah 55:10-11
- Certainty of a victorious outcome. Romans 8:28

October 21

OUR RESPONSIBILITY

- A strong desire for spiritual maturity. Job 27:10; Psalm 73:25; Philippians 3:8-9
- To call on the Lord for help. Psalm 145:18; Jeremiah 29:13; 33:3
- To yield completely to His guidance. Psalm 37:5; Proverbs 3:5-6; 16:3
- To confess and cleanse all impurities. Psalm 51:1-12; 1 John 1:9
- To accept circumstances that cannot be changed. Philippians 4:11
- To keep the defenses up. Ephesians 6:13-18
- To be filled with the Holy Spirit. Ephesians 5:18
- To apply the Word. Psalm 119
- To rest on faith. Hebrews 11:6

October 22

AN EXAMPLE OF ABRAHAM

When he was called, he obeyed. Hebrews 11:8
When he received a promise, he believed. Hebrews 11:9-11
When he was blessed, he shared. Genesis 13:9
When he was burdened, he prayed. Genesis 18:23-32
When he was tested he trusted. Genesis 22:8; Hebrews 11:17-19

October 23

RESPONSES TO MARITAL CONFLICTS

- *FLEE* - Opting for separation and divorce.
- *FIGHT* - Each insisting on his or her rights.
- *FAKE* - Pretending that everything is OK. Keeping things inside.
- *FLOW* - Peaceful coexistence without any closeness.
- *FLY* - Soaring to new dimensions.
    - Confess the mistakes and repent. James 5:16
    - Release all expectations, rights, ties and strings. Matthew 5:38-42
    - Forgive others and yourself. Matthew 18:21-22; Romans 8:1
    - Pick up the cross of self-denial. Matthew 16:24
    - Acknowledge and submit to the headship of the husband. Ephesians 5:22-24
    - Take refuge in Christ. Matthew 11:28-30

October 24

TO BUILD A GOOD MARRIAGE

- God must be the foundation.
- Commitment consists of the beams and nails that hold the structure together.
- Unity is a leakproof roof, consisting of forgiveness, trust and loyalty.
- Love that is unconditional and unselfish provides the light, warmth, security and beauty that transform a house into a home.
- Give up the idea of a perfect marriage.
- Love is a commitment and involves the will.
- Give more affection and praise than criticism.
- Abandon all attempts to change your partner by criticism.
- Become aware of the unique needs of your partner.
- Settle the differences and forgive any hurt before going to bed at night.
- Establish a prayer life.
- Seek help first from God.

October 25

THREE WAYS TO LIVE

Colorful - We can enjoy it. John 15:11; Philippians 4:4

     Gray - We can exist with no sense of direction. Proverbs 4:26; 29:18

          Black - We can endure it in misery until it is all over. Job 7:1-21

October 26

CONTROLLED EATING

- Remember your one and only goal in life: To please God.
- When tempted, call on the name of Jesus and STOP -
    Surrender – Trust - Obey - Praise.
- Never eat in secret.
- Plan ahead what and how much to eat.
- Never eat standing up.
- Distinguish between hunger and lust by listening to your stomach, not your
    emotions, nerves or tastebuds.
- Eat very slowly.
- Determine your average calorie intake once a month.
- Weigh yourself once a week.
- Remember that you <u>always</u> have a choice whether to eat or not.
- Keep an honest and accurate record of your spiritual, mental and physical commitments.

October 27

TO WALK THE TALK

What messages do I send to others?

Do they see the <u>LOVE</u> of God in me, or my criticism and unforgiveness? His unchanging <u>JOY</u> or my foul moods? His <u>PEACE</u> or my fears, anxieties and complaints? His <u>PATIENCE</u> or my short fuse? His <u>GENTLENESS</u> or my unkindness? His <u>INTEGRITY</u> or my dishonesty? His <u>FAITHFULNESS</u> or my disloyalty? His <u>HUMILITY</u> or my pride His <u>SELF-CONTROL</u> or my gluttony?

October 28

A PROFILE OF JESUS

The Lord Jesus Christ represents genuine humanity combined with full deity.

He who is the Bread of Life began His ministry hungering. He who is the Water of Life ended His ministry thirsting. He was poor, yet He fed the multitudes. He was weary, yet He is our rest. He was called a devil, yet He cast out demons. He prayed, yet He answers prayers. He wept, yet He dries our tears. He was sold for 30 pieces of silver, yet He redeems sinners. He was led as a lamb to the slaughter, yet He is the Good Shepherd. He gave His life, yet by dying He destroyed death.

October 29

SATAN'S TARGETS

Satan targets the minds of people, because if he has your mind, he has you.

- Philosophies indoctrinate our minds to convert us to their thinking.
- Advertisers bombard our minds to get our money.
- Politicians try to manipulate our minds so we vote for them.
- Education undermines discernment by erasing the distinction between good and evil, right and wrong.
- Liberal arts infiltrate our minds by books like "Harry Potter", pictures like pornography, music like Hard Rock and Rap, movies, videos and TV shows that are loaded with sex and violence.

Genesis 3:4-5

REINCARNATION - "You surely shall not die." I determine my own destiny.
ESOTERICISM - "Your eyes will be opened." I have all enlightenment there is.
PANTHEISM - "You will be like God." I am God and therefore self-sufficient.
RELATIVISM - "You will know good and evil." I determine my own morals.

Isaiah 14:13-14

"I will ascend to heaven and rule. I will take the highest throne. I will be like the Most High."

October 30

SATAN'S STRATEGIES

- He directs your attention to a deep need or desire in order to give you what he wants you to have.
- He chooses a time of temptation when you are most vulnerable.
    HALT - Don't let yourself get too hungry, too angry, too lonely or too tired.
- He creates doubts by misinterpreting or rationalizing the Word of God.
- He gets you to confide in him instead of praying, and to seek counsel from anybody except God.
- He deceives you about the dire consequences of yielding to him.
- He creates divisions between family and church members.
- He defiles your testimony and witness.
- He ultimately destroys your peace, joy, happiness and contentment.

October 31

HALLOWEEN - A PARTY FOR SATAN
Deuteronomy 18:10-14

Why should Christians give tribute to Satan on this unholy "Hell-o-ween" with all it's evil symbols? It would be totally inappropriate for Hindus to celebrate Passover or for Jews to celebrate Ramadan.

All Halloween decorations represent something demonic or occult. The "Jack o' Lantern" is an ancient symbol of the damned soul. The black cat is associated with witchcraft and superstitions. Dragons are seen as Satan's helpmates. A spider lies in wait to trap you in it's web. Ghosts are believed to be restless spirits on a mission of revenge.

There are no ghosts or haunted houses. The spirits of Christians will be in the presence of the Lord Jesus Christ when they die. 2.Corinthians 5:8. The spirits of the unsaved are confined to Hades, the abode of the dead, and cannot come back to earth. Luke 16:26.

Of course, putting on a sheet will not turn a child into a ghost any more than putting on a mask will turn an adult into a pumpkin. Yet when children engage in such practices, they often lose a healthy respect for that which is evil.

Times have changed. Children and adults are more susceptible to evil influences because of the deteriorating standards in society. When moral confusion abounds, a little unwholesome entertainment can be devastating.

November 1

SALVATION IN A NUTSHELL

RECOGNIZE GOD'S PLAN - God loves you and wants you to experience His peace and eternal life. John 3:16

REALIZE THE PROBLEM - People choose to disobey God and go their own way. This results in separation from God. Romans 3:23

RESPOND TO GOD'S REMEDY - God sent His Son to bridge the gap. Christ paid the penalty for our sins when He died on the Cross and rose from the grave. Romans 5:8

RECEIVE GOD'S SON - You cross the bridge into God's family when you ask Christ to be your Lord and Savior. John 1:12

November 2

THE WAY TO GOD

A walk through the Old Testament Tabernacle. Exodus 25-27; 30-31; 35-40

- *THE GATE* - Entering with thanksgiving and praise. Psalm 100:4
-
- *THE BRONZE ALTAR* - Salvation secured by Christ's ultimate sacrifice.
        Isaiah 53:5-6; 2 Corinthians 5:21

- *THE BRONZE BASIN* - Confession and cleansing.
        Psalm 139:23-24; 2 Corinthians 7:1; 1 John 1:9

- *THE DOOR* - Christ as the Way, the Truth and the Life. John 14:6
-
- *THE BREAD* - The Body of Christ for strength and sustenance. John 6:35
-
- *THE LAMPSTAND* - The Holy Spirit to guide us in the dark world.
        Psalm 119:105; John 8:12

- *THE GOLDEN ALTAR* - A place for prayer and intercession.
        Hebrews 4:16; 10:19-22

- *THE MERCY SEAT* - The inside of the Holy of Holies where God communes
        *w*ith His people.

November 3

WAYS TO SERVE GOD

RESPONSE TO A NEED - Religion, zeal and self-motivation tend to work <u>FOR </u>God.
    Most of it is in the flesh. This takes place in the "Outer Courts."

RESPONSE TO A PERSONAL CALLING - Hardships can bring us to the Yoke of Jesus
    to learn from Him. We are taught to work <u>WITH </u>Him in the "Holy Place."

RESPONSE TO THE PRESENCE OF GOD - We begin to yearn to work <u>UNTO</u> Him in
    worship in the "Holy of Holies."

READY TO BE A DISCIPLE - We leave the Tabernacle and go out into the world to
    work <u>FOR, WITH,</u> and <u>UNTO</u> God, so we can touch the lives of others.

"EMPLOYED" BY GOD

- *JOB DESCRIPTION -*
    The location is anywhere.
    The duty is 24 hours a day, 7 days a week.
    The duration is for the rest of your life.
    To be available to serve God in any way He pleases. Isaiah 6:8
    To live entirely by faith. 2 Corinthians 5:7; Hebrews 11:1, 6
    To function in the spirit, not in the flesh or by willpower.
        Romans 6:11; 7:14-25; 8:14; Galatians 5:1-6
    To submit to the leading of the Holy Spirit.
        Psalm 143:10; Proverbs 16:9; 19:21
    To focus on God alone. Josh 22:5;
        Joshua 22:5; 1 Corinthians 10:31; 2 Cor 5:15; Colossians 3:17, 23

- *SALARY -*
    Grace. Psalm 23; 2 Corinthians 12:9
    Guaranteed security. John 14:16-18; 1 John 4:4
    Material needs are met. Psalm 34:9-10; Matthew 6:33; Philippians 4:19
    Strength. Isaiah 40:31; Philippians 4:13
    Inner satisfaction. Psalms 37:4; 107:9; Isaiah 58:11; Jeremiah 31:14
    Peace. Psalm 29:11; Isaiah 26:3; John 14:27; 16:33; Philippians 4:7
    Crown of glory.
        1 Corinthians 9:25; 2 Timothy 4:8; James 1:12; 1 Peter 5:4; Rev 2:10

- *BENEFITS -*
    More responsibilities, challenges and satisfaction for a job well done.
    Wider opportunities to love, praise and worship God.
    Greater capacity to enjoy heaven.
    Deeply satisfying fellowships in the Body of Christ.
    The heights of joy on this earth will be eclipsed in heaven.
    Eternal life in the immediate presence of the triune God.

- *PENSION -*
    To live in the perfect bliss of heaven forever.
    Psalm 73:24; John 14:1-3; 1 Thessalonians 4:17; Revelation 21:4

When seeking employment in this world, it is more important what you have achieved, than what you are. In serving God, the number one priority is who you are rather than what you achieve.

Discipleship is more than a full-time job -
it is a way of life.

November 5

HANDPICKED BY GOD

ENOCH -	To walk with God for fellowship.
NOAH -	To prepare the ark.
ABRAHAM -	To walk by faith.
ISAAC -	To live the life of a son.
JACOB -	To establish a nation.
MOSES -	To lead God's people out of Egypt.
JOSHUA -	To conquer the enemies.
RUTH -	To portray loyalty and faithfulness.
SAMUEL -	To admonish others.
DAVID -	To praise and worship.
SOLOMON -	To display God's rich blessings.
ISAIAH -	To prophesy.
JEREMIAH -	To warn others.
DANIEL -	To be a witness.
JOHN the BAPTIST -	To pave the way for Christ.
MARY -	To bear and rear God's Son.
MATTHEW -	To present Christ, the King, to the Jews.
MARK -	To present Christ, the Servant, to the Romans.
LUKE -	To present Christ, the Man, to the Greeks.
JOHN -	To present the deity of Christ to the world.
PAUL -	To evangelize the world and set up churches.
STEPHEN -	To be a martyr for his beliefs.
PETER -	To preach the Gospel.
AQUILA and PRISCILLA -	To minister behind the scenes.
ME -	???

November 6

BEING YOKED WITH JESUS
Matthew 11:28-30

By sticking your head in His yoke, you will begin to learn His ways.

If you try to go ahead of Him, you get sore shoulders.
If you refuse to move, you get sore ears.
If you turn, you get chafed.

Just go along for a walk with Him and enjoy His presence.

November 7

WORRY

DEFINITION OF WORRY -

Worry is distrust in God's promises. It is faith in the negative. It is belief in defeat.

Worry is <u>irreverent</u>. It fails to honor the fact that God is sovereign.
Worry is <u>irrelevant</u>. It does not change what will or will not happen.
Worry is <u>irresponsible</u>. It is a waste of time and energy.

PROTECTION FROM WORRY -

- Practice the presence of God. When worry appears, let the Lord confront it.
     Joshua 1:9; Isaiah 41:10; Mark 10:27; 1 John 4:4
- Make your prayers specific. Philippians 4:6-7; James 4:3
- Claim the promises of God. There are 7474 in the Bible.
     Isaiah 45:2; Romans 4:21; Titus 1:2; 2 Peter 1:4
- Wait with patience for God's assurance. Psalm 27:14; Isaiah 40:31; Romans 8:25
- Praise God for His sovereignty. Whatever happens, <u>IT IS OK</u>.

Today is the Tomorrow
you worried about
Yesterday.

November 8

ANGER

DEFINITION OF ANGER -

- Mild irritation - Discomfort for the ego.
- Indignation - Reaction to a sin or injustice that needs to be expressed.
- Wrath - Strong desire for revenge.
- Fury - Irrational violence.
- Rage - Loss of self-control and sanity.

ANGER IS JUSTIFIED -

- When the Creator is spurned. Romans 1:19-23
- When people knowingly and openly disobey God's Word.
     Exodus 32:19; 1 Kings 11:9-10
- When justice is perverted. Isaiah 5:20-23

November 9

A COUNSELLING SESSION WITH GOD

When something is out of sync in your life, find a quiet corner and pour out your heart.

* Frustration and bitterness for being misunderstood, ignored, opposed, rejected and falsely accused.

ANSWER - Delegate the problem to the Cross for forgiveness, the Risen Christ for comfort, strength and wisdom and the Glorified Christ for justice.

* Desiring my own fulfillment in life.

ANSWER - Everything is the work of the flesh if done apart from the specific leading of the Holy Spirit.

* Regret over having missed my true vocation.

ANSWER - My ultimate plan for your life is your sanctification and conformity to the image of Christ. A life of true devotion can be lived anywhere, anytime, regardless of outer circumstances.

* Desire to die soon to be with the Lord.

ANSWER - The longer you live, the longer your light will shine in this dark world, the more opportunities you will have to express your gratitude to Jesus for saving you, and the greater your reward will be in heaven.

* Upset with disruptions of my schedules and plans.

ANSWER - Submit to the living, flexible, vibrant, all-knowing Holy Spirit. True freedom is only secured by yielding to my plan for you.

* Hurt over being left out, side-lined, by-passed, unemployed, retired.

ANSWER - Be faithful in your given assignment. Meet the challenge of the ordinary and the difficult by abiding in my love and persevering in praise.

November 10

WHAT IS PRAYER ?

Prayer is living in continual God-consciousness, in which everything we see and experience becomes a deep awareness of and surrender to our heavenly Father. We bring a temptation before God and ask for His help. When we experience something good, we immediately thank the Lord for it. When we see evil around us, we ask God to make it right and allow us to help, if such involvement is according to His will. When we meet people who do not know Christ, we pray for God to draw them to Himself and to use us as faithful witnesses. When we encounter trouble, we turn to God as our Deliverer.

* Prayer brings us into the *PRESENCE* of God. Deuteronomy 4:29
* Prayer connects us to the *POWER* of God. Philippians 4:13
* Prayer unveils the *PURPOSE* of God. James 1:5
* Prayer clarifies the *PROMISES* of God. Isaiah 42:16

November 11

PITFALLS IN LEARNING

- By intuition, which some call spiritual discernment.

DANGER - Insight may come from our own fallen nature, from the world or
from Satan himself, resulting in confusion and deception.
2 Corinthians 11:14; 1 Timothy 4:1; 1 John 4:1

- By listening to, believing and following so-called "spirit-filled" leaders.

DANGER - They may be deceived themselves.
Matthew 7:21; 1 Timothy 6:20-21; 2 Timothy 3:5-7

- By following the teachings of an established, organized church.

DANGER - The church doctrine may contain error. Galatians 1:6-9

- By comparing Scripture with Scripture in many translations and languages.

DANGER - Accumulation of intellectual head knowledge.
2 Corinthians 3:6; 2 Timothy 2:14

November 12

THE PERFECT MAN

Jesus integrates all aspects of a balanced, harmonious personhood. (See June 16)

SANGUINE - Great capacity for love and joy, cheerful, warm, forgiving, optimistic,
creative, resourceful, expressive, flexible, intuitive, extrovert, fun.

CHOLERIC - Great capacity for leadership, strong, practical, energetic, courageous,
adventurous, positive, outspoken, decisive, tenacious, industrious, cool,
disciplined, exudes confidence, excels in emergencies.

MELANCHOLIC - Great capacity for spiritual understanding, sensitive, dependable,
considerate, thoughtful, faithful, loyal, devoted, respectful, humble,
obedient, persistent, compassionate, discerning, orderly, analytical,
self-sacrificing, introvert.

PHLEGMATIC - Great capacity for peace and contentment, kind, controlled, consistent,
steadfast, patient, submissive, modest, relaxed, pleasant, observant,
balanced, available, trustworthy, sense of humor, calm, collected.

November 13

FORGIVENESS IS A MANDATE

Forgiveness is a firm commandment of God. Any violations result in the sin of disobedience and rebellion with all it's consequences.

- We have to forgive others, even when they don't deserve it. Romans 5:6,8
- We have to forgive, even when they don't ask for it. Matthew 5:23-24
- We have to forgive, even when they don't admit any wrongdoing.
     Mark 2:5; 1 Corinthians 4:5
- We have to forgive, even when we suffer by the sins of others.
     Isaiah 53:5, 12; Matthew 18:21-22
- We have to forgive, even when they keep on prospering.
     Psalms 37:7; 73:3; Romans 12:15, 17, 19

November 14

FORGIVENESS MADE POSSIBLE

- By our perfect trust in the righteousness of God's justice.
     Psalms 119:137, 164; 145:17; Jeremiah 9:24; 2 Thessalonians 1:6-9
- By submitting to the sovereignty of God.
     Deuteronomy 4:35, 39; Psalm 135:5-6; Isaiah 45:5-7
- By the fact that we have been forgiven.
     Matthew 18:23-35; Ephesians 4:32; Coossians 3:13
- By the fact that our destiny cannot be altered by evil forces.
     Jeremiah 29:11; Philippians 1:6
- By the fact that persecutions actually help to attain spiritual maturity.
     Genesis 50:20; Psalm 119:71; James 1:2-4
- By focusing on our own reward instead of the punishment of the offender.
     Psalm 58:11; Proverbs 11:18; 2 Corinthians 5:10; 2 Timothy 4:7-8
- By recognizing the ignorance of the offender.
     Luke 23:34; Acts 7:60; 1 Timothy 1:13
- By understanding why some people behave the way they do.
     Psalm 103:14; Matthew 7:1-5
- By contrasting the present temporary suffering and injustice to the future eternal joy.
     Psalm 103:15-18; Romans 8:18; 1 Corinthians 2:9; 2 Corinthians 4:17
- By comparing your hurts with the sufferings of Christ.
- By remembering all the blessings from the Lord that the other person might not have.
- By looking for the good and positive points in the other person.
- By praying for the one who has hurt you.
- By seeking an opportunity to show kindness to that person.
- By releasing him from your grip and let him go.

November 15

EQUIPPED FOR SPIRITUAL WARFARE
Ephesians 6:14-18

Put on the whole armor of God before getting up in the morning.

* *BELT OF TRUTH* - Protection against deception and compromise.
        Two plus two <u>always</u> equals four.

* *BREASTPLATE OF RIGHTEOUSNESS* - Protection against self-righteousness
        and pride, low self-esteem and depression.

* *SHOES* - Protection against weariness and discouragement in our walk on God's path.

* *SHIELD OF FAITH* - Protection from the fiery darts of doubts about God's
        perfect love and infinite wisdom, and fear that God is not in absolute control.

* *HELMET OF SALVATION* - Protection against the assaults on the threefold
    Salvation package that consists of the cancellation of sin's penalty at the Cross, the strength
    to withstand the power of sin in the present, and the promise of the complete removal of the
    presence of sin in the future.

* *SWORD OF THE SPIRIT* - God's Word to be used against all attacks from the
        world, the flesh and the devil.

* *PRAYER* - Open communication with God through repentance, supplication and praise.

November 16

TO SAIL OR RIDE

Now that the armor is on, we get up and go to work.

Launch a sailboat in the sea and rig up the sails. We cannot create the wind, but we can set up the sails to catch it when it comes.

Tack up a horse.
    Dressage - Preparation by studying, meditating and praying.
    Cross-Country - Perseverance by meeting the challenges and not quitting.
    Stadium-Jumping - Performance by producing excellence.

November 17

ASK YOURSELF

- *WHO AM I ?*

  I am a created being with a body, soul and spirit, accountable to my Creator for my attitude, action and assets.

  Genesis 1:27; 2:7; Matthew 12:36; Romans 14:12

- *WHY AM I HERE ?*

  To get acquainted with my Creator by faith. 2 Corinthians 5:7; Philippians 3:10

  To prepare for the eternal life to come. Matthew 6:19-20

  To develop the wisdom to know what can and cannot be changed. 1 Kings 3:9

  To chart a course and purpose in life. Proverbs 4:23-27

  To put the plan into action. James 2:17, 26

  To be a channel for God's love, joy and peace to others. John 13:34-35

- *WHAT DO I HAVE ?*

  I have complete freedom to choose my inner attitude, but certain limitations to change my outer circumstances.

  Joshua 24:15; James 4:13-15

- *WHAT SHOULD I DO ?*

  Time in this life is limited. Death is certain. There is a reason for every experience. Joy and sorrow come and go. Stay in the will of God and fill every moment with quality and meaning.

  Ecclesiastes 3:1-8; Matt 6:19-20; 1 Cor 15:58; Ephesians 5:15-17; Hebr 9:27

November 18

WHOM SHOULD I PLEASE ?

We all have three choices where our focus should be.

- To please self - I, me, mine, myself. Isaiah 53:6; 56:11; Philippians 2:21
- To please others - Works of the flesh, do-gooders. Isaiah 64:6; Matthew 7:22-23
- To please God - Obedience to His Word. 1 Cor 10:31; Phil 1:21; Hebrews 11:6

Keep the commandments.

Tune in to the Holy Spirit.

Follow God's directives.

Check your motives.

November 19

TO DO OR TO BE

The difference between achievements or Christ-likeness.

There is a giant eraser following your footsteps that will eventually wipe out all visible and material traces of your works here on earth. The only accomplishment that will last for eternity, is the transformation of your character from a born sinner, separated from God, to a born-again child of God who has been conformed to the image of Jesus Christ. Therefore what we <u>do</u> should become a means of what we should <u>be</u>.

Select work and activities that will enhance your development towards Christ-likeness.
In the final analysis it is not important <u>what</u> we do, but <u>why</u> we do it, <u>how</u> we do it and for <u>whom</u> we do it.

November 20

JOB OR VOCATION

How to turn your occupation into a mission.

There are only two kinds of work -
>   *Secular work* when done for self or any other reason.
>   *Sacred work* when done as unto Christ.

•   View your work as a tool, a steppingstone and a bridge for your divine calling.

•   View your job as an opportunity to serve your true Master, Jesus Christ.
    Christianity helps us to face the music, even when we don't like the tune.
    Sour notes can be caused by a nasty boss, obnoxious co-workers, poor working conditions or an inadequate salary. But a sense of vocation will override the dissonance by looking for ways to serve Christ in the difficulty. Don't let any occupational dissatisfaction rob you of your joy in your calling.

•   View the salary, profits and benefits as a by-product of a job well done in the eyes of God. The eternal rewards far outweigh the temporary job satisfaction.

Colossians 3:17

"Whatever you do – no matter what it is – in word or deed,
do everything in the name of the Lord Jesus,
giving praise to God the Father through Him.

November 21

MY PERSONAL TEN COMMANDMENTS

- *Joshua 22:5* "To love the Lord, my God, to walk in all His ways, to keep His commandments, to cling unto Him and to serve Him with all my heart, spirit, soul and body."
- *Psalm 19:14* "To let the words of my mouth and the meditations of my heart be acceptable to God."
- *Psalm 34:1* "To thank the Lord and praise Him at all times."
- *Proverbs 3:5-6* "To trust the Lord with all my heart and acknowledge His sovereignty in all situations."
- *Matthew 6:33* "To seek the Kingdom of God and His righteousness first."
- *Matthew 7:12* "To do to others what I want them to do to me."
- *Romans 12:2* "To be conformed to Christ, not to the world."
- *Colossians 3:17* "Everything I do must glorify God."
- *2 Corinthians 5:9* "To be well-pleasing to God at all times."
- *2 Timothy 4:7* "To hang in there and keep my faith."

November 22

PEARLS AND SNOWFLAKES

<u>Turning an irritation into an inspiration.</u>

An ugly impurity or a nagging irritation found in an oyster becomes a precious pearl by being covered my multiple layers of a substance called "Mother of Pearl."

Submission. Matthew 26:39. Forgiveness. Matthew 18:21-22.

Love. 1 Peter 4:8. Thanksgiving. Ephesians 5:20. Praise. Psalms 34:1; 103:1

<u>The lesson of the snowflake.</u>

Some snowflakes glitter like diamonds; others resemble delicate lace doilies. Although all snowflakes are different from each other, they share remarkable similarities. Every snowflake has six points. They are made up of molecules of hydrogen and oxygen and are symmetrical. They come into existence because at the center of each one is a tiny bit of foreign matter. It may be as small as one 100'000th of a millimeter in size. Yet it must be there for a snowflake to form.

And so can hardships and tragedies in life provide the substance for God to turn them into something beautiful, as the pearl, the snowflake and the mature Christian.

November 23

THANKSGIVING AND PRAISE

The hardest thing that is ever required of us Christians, is to thank and praise God <u>in and for</u> everything. That includes problems, calamities and disasters of every sort with one and <u>only</u> exception - *SIN* . That needs to be confessed and forsaken.

The Holy Spirit will give us the discernment what to confess and for what to praise God. To the outside world, praise in adversity is utterly ridiculous, to the faith it is the most demanding form of prayer. But without doubt, it is the most formidable weapon we have against Satan. It snaps all power and dominion away from him, because praise acknowledges the power of a sovereign, holy, loving and trustworthy God.

Praise is not presumptuous like some of the prayers for healing, because it does not demand anything from God, but instead submits joyfully to the will of God. That is when true peace floods our hearts, and we <u>know</u> that we are in God's loving hands regardless of outer circumstances.

The Bible predicts that as Christians we will face a lot of persecutions and hardships in this sin-sick world. If God did not allow His own to be tested, Satan could raise the same complaints as he did regarding Job. "Would Job worship you if he got nothing out of it? You have always protected him, his family and his possession." Job 1: 9-10

When God permits Satan to take away our loved ones, possessions and health, He does it only to prove to Satan that we are truly God's children. So we can be a tremendous witness, if we stand up for God and praise Him in the midst of "sackcloth and ashes." Then Satan is put to shame, and he has nothing to accuse us for. And that really makes him mad !!

November 24

DOES THIS SOUND FAMILIAR ?

<u>Six reasons for the judgment of Israel</u> - Isaiah 5:8-23

- Greed and irresponsible depletion of natural resources.
- Drunkenness and pleasure-seeking.
- Sinning without shame.
- Reversal of God's standards for right and wrong.
- Pride and self-righteousness.
- Justification of the guilty and persecution of the innocent.

U S A , TAKE HEED, LEST YE FALL

November 25

THE APOSTLE PAUL ON LOVE
1 Corinthians 13:4-8

Love is long-suffering and patient with people.
Love is kind, understanding, compassionate and void of criticism.
Love does not envy. There are two kinds of envy - one covets the possession of other
      people; the other begrudges the fact that others prosper.
Love is not self-promoting and does not brag about anything.
Love is not proud and inflated with it's own importance.
Love is not ill-mannered. What you are speaks louder than what you say.
Love is not self-seeking. Christians have no rights, only privileges.
Love is not easily irritated or provoked to anger.
Love does not hold grudges for any wrong it has received.
Love is grieved with sin and finds no pleasure in anything that is wrong.
Love rejoices in the Truth and in God's righteousness.
Love accepts unfair treatments without desiring retaliation.
Love believes in God's goodness and the best in other people. When love has no
      evidence, it believes the best. When the evidence is adverse, it hopes for the best.
Love trusts in all things that the Truth will prevail.
Love endures all things, not in passive resignation, but with a song of praise.
Love is eternal, complete, permanent and everlasting.

November 26

WISE ADVICE

If I am a Christian, and I am complaining and grumbling, the world doesn't know that I am different from any pagan. My spirituality is gone, my testimony has departed, and my effect in dispelling the darkness in this world has flown the coop, because I have chosen to magnify the problem instead of magnifying the answer by praising God.

One thing God cannot stand is murmuring and complaining. When we complain, find faults or react in other negative ways to the blessings of God, we drain the life right out of ourselves. A foolproof recipe for a "do-it-yourself-destruction" is - gripe your head off and complain your heart out.

God will do what He wants to do. Let's not fall into the trap of thinking that God and I can do something. Pretty soon I'll think that I and God can do something. The next step will be to think that I am the indispensable partner, rendering God helpless without me.
God doesn't need our self-promoting help, He needs our submission to His directions.

November 27

THE PURPOSE OF TESTING

JOB's test was necessary to reveal his self-righteousness. Job 27-29; 42:6

PETER's test was necessary to reveal his self-confidence. Luke 22:33

HEZEKIAH's test was to reveal his self-sufficiency and bad judgment. 2 Chron 32:31

THE ISRAELITES' 40 years in the wilderness was to reveal their lack of faith. Deut 8:2-5

OUR TESTING -
* To prove our loyalty to God.
* To purge our hearts, purify our lives and burn out the dross by fire.
    Psalm 66:10-12; Isaiah 1:25; 48:10; Ezekiel 22:17-22
* To bring our weaknesses to the surface to be transformed by the Holy Spirit.
* To fine-tune us to the voice of God.
* To draw us closer to Him.
* To be witnesses to the world. 2 Corinthians 4:10-18

JESUS in the wilderness. To prove to His followers and to the world that He is beyond reproach.

November 28

OUR SINFUL NATURE

Our sinful nature resembles a tree. The different branches are selfishness, unbelief, pride, greed, disobedience, self-pity, ingratitude, rebellion and hate. The branches can be cut off, but they always grow back.

What we need is to pull the whole filthy and ungodly tree up by it's roots and destroy it. Jesus died not only for our sins, but for our whole sinful nature.

God commands us to be holy. Leviticus 20:7. Jesus tells us to be perfect. Matthew 5:48. The very fact that holiness and perfection are required from us, is proof that it is available to those who believe. Then we become branches of the Vine and are connected to the life-giving sap. That is when the Holy Spirit indwells us and produce wholesome fruit. Works of the flesh stem from our sinful nature and God will not accept it's fruit.

GRACE

<u>G</u> - God's <u>R</u> - riches <u>A</u> - at <u>C</u> - Christ's <u>E</u> - expense

November 29

WORKS IN THE FLESH

- To perform works without love. 1 Corinthians 13:1-3
- Works without faith. Romans 14:23
- Works without joy. Deuteronomy 28:47-48
- Works from the old nature. Colossians 3:5-9
- Works from selfish motives. Ecclesiastes 2:4-11
- Works by our own righteousness. Isaiah 64:6
- Works by our own labor. Genesis 4:2-5
- Works without consulting God. Isaiah 30:1-2
- Works without the full approval of the husband. Ephesians 5:22
- Works to serve the wrong master. Matthew 7:21-23
- Works to appeal to legalism. Galatians 2:16; Colossians 2:20-23
- Works using perishable material. 1 Corinthians 3:11-13

November 30

WORKS BY THE SPIRIT

- In agreement with the Word.
- Obedience to the "Still Small Voice".
- Motive must be to glorify God.
- Love, joy and peace must be present.
- All credit goes to God.

December 1

A NEW BEGINNING

- Close the door on your past. Philippians 3:13-14
- Set time aside for spiritual instruction and prayer. Mark 1:35
- Perform the daily tasks with joy and diligence. 1 Corinthians 10:31
- Relinquish all your possessions and become a caretaker of God's creation. Ps 24:1
- Pray faithfully for family and friends. 1 Samuel 12:23; Romans 1:9
- Bring forth the Fruit of the Spirit by abiding in Christ. John 15:4-8
- Look at your life on this earth from the viewpoint of eternity. 1 Corinthians 4:5
    Your Past. Isaiah 61:3
            Your present. Psalm 118:24; Matthew 6:33
                    Your future. Isaiah 64:4; Romans 8:18; Revelation 21:4-7

ANSWERING QUESTIONS
1 Peter 3:15-16

What is your number one goal in life?

          To serve and please God. Joshua 22:5; 2 Corinthians 5:9

          To strive towards maturity. Matthew 5:48; Ephesians 4:13-15

          To be a blessing to others. Romans 15:2; Philippians 2:3-5

How do you reach that goal?

          To use the Bible as a roadmap and handbook to live by. Psalm 119

          To stay in close contact with God by prayer. Psalms 16:8; 63:1-8

          To put into practice what I learn. James 1:22

Why do you want to please God rather than yourself?

          I want to show my gratitude to the One who has loved me so much as to save me.

Aren't you in bondage to legalism?

          Even though I am a servant, I am free and do as I please, because keeping the commandments is what I <u>want</u> to do, not what I <u>have</u> to do. John 8:32; 14:15

Do you enjoy life?

          I regard the life here on earth as a transition period, an education for a higher vocation, a "boot camp" for spiritual fitness, the engagement before the wedding and a time for investing treasures in heaven. Romans 8:18

How do you cope with adversity?

          The quality of life depends for 10% on circumstances and 90% on attitude. I have a choice how to respond to anything that comes my way. I welcome any challenge as a stepping stone towards spiritual maturity. 1 Thessalonians 5:16-18

What is the cost of discipleship?

          A true believer signs up for life. Discipleship means to let go of personal ambitions and do without physical and emotional comfort if called upon. There has to be a willingness to suffer daily for Christ's sake and follow Him wherever He leads. Luke 9:23

A bird is free in the air, but place him in the water and he will die. A fish is free in the water, but leave him on the dry sand and he will perish. So the Christian is free when he does the will of God and is obedient to His commands. This is as natural a realm for a child of God as the air is for the bird or the water for the fish.

          True freedom is not having our own way -
          it can only be found in yielding to God's way.

December 3

PSALM 81 ON PRAISE

REASONS FOR PRAISE -

- God commands it. Praise initiates true worship. The way to the Holy Place leads through the Courts of praise. The mandatory Feast Days in Israel were occasions for praise. (Verse 4)
- Praise is a witness and a testimony to the world of the sovereignty and ultimate goodness of God. (Verse 5)
- Praise expresses our gratitude for salvation and deliverance from bondage and slavery. (Verse 6)
- Praise acknowledges that God answers prayers. (Verse 7a and b)
- Praise confirms God's love even while He tests, disciplines and chastens. (Verse 7c)

BENEFITS FOR PRAISE -

- Protection from satanic influences. High praise is the most powerful weapon against the kingdom of darkness. (Verse 9a)
- Purity of worship. The focus on God's sovereignty leaves no room for any other power. (Verse 9b)
- Personal relationship with God. He is our God, and He wants us to be His people. (Verse 10a)
- Manifestation of grace. He gives us freely what we cannot produce ourselves, so we can offer it back to Him in the form of faith, love and praise. (Verse 10b)
- Enemies subdued. They will no longer harass us, so we can walk and rest in peace. (Verse 14a)
- Adversaries avenged. God will deal personally with our adversaries. Battles and vengeance belong to God. (Verse 14b)
- Assurance of lasting victories. Line up with God. (Verse 15a)
- Provisions for all our needs. We will be well taken care of. (Verse 16a)
- Complete satisfaction. God fulfills the deepest longings of our souls. (Verse 16b)

REQUIREMENTS FOR PRAISE -

- Acknowledgment of the Lordship of God. Function of the <u>spirit.</u> Job 1:12
- Getting to know God and His ways. Function of the <u>mind.</u>
    Romans 12:2; Ephesians 4:23-24; Colossians 3:10
- Unconditional surrender to God's authority. Function of the <u>will.</u>
    Matthew 26:39; 2 Corinthians 10:5; James 4:7
- Serving God with gladness and joy. Function of the <u>emotions.</u> Deuteronomy 28:47
- True worship. Function of the <u>spirit, soul and body.</u>
    Isaiah 6:1-4; Revelation 4:8

December 4

CONTENTMENT

The reason so many people are unhappy today and seeking help to cope with life is that they fail to understand what human existence is all about. Until we recognize that life is not just something to be enjoyed, but rather a task that each of us is assigned to, we will never find meaning in our lives, and we'll never be truly happy.

Contentment is a product of a heart resting in God, the outcome of my will brought into the subjection of the divine will. Contentment is possible only as we maintain the attitude of accepting everything that enters our lives as coming from the hand of Him who is too wise to err and too loving to cause one of His children a needless tear. Real contentment is possible only by being in the presence of the Lord Jesus Christ.

Christian growth comes through relentless perseverance of applying and obeying spiritual principles.

When we get bored, we may not need a change or an outside stimulation, but to settle down and learn to deal with the "challenge of the ordinary".

A decision we make today is like a rock tossed in the pond of tomorrow -
the consequences are rippling through our future days, months, years and decades.

December 5

A QUESTIONNAIRE

Before making important decisions, ask yourself -

- Am I on the right track?
- Am I investing in lasting values?
- Am I building with gold, silver and precious stones, or with wood, hay and stubble?
- What is my number one priority at this point and time in my life?
- What are my possibilities and options?
- What do I personally desire and prefer?
- What are my innermost motives behind these desires?
- What are the pros and the cons?
- Is my goal feasible and realistic?
- What are the demands on my physical strength, energy, emotions, time and money?
- In the circumstances that I find myself right <u>now,</u> what would I do, if I had only six more months or 30 more years to live?
- Will this decision help or hinder me to grow in the image of Christ?

December 6

TRAPPED

Closed doors can seem like insurmountable cliffs or vast chasms. For most of His children, God's hedges do not entail suffering, but only protection. For some, however, they mean unending pain and weakness, disappointment and sorrow in varying degrees, up to total imprisonment. Why this must be so we may not know. Sufficient for us is the fact that God Himself has hedged us in, and God's boundaries are always for our good.

God, who lives with us and in us in the form of the Holy Spirit, longs to make our thorny wall a thing of wonder to men, angels and demons - a thing that will one day bring forth radiant blossoms and luscious fruit. How can that be? Did not the thorniest tree of all bring forth the holy flower of redemption?

If God has entrusted you with a hedge of suffering or a closed door, let Him teach you how to live so that His purpose for love and compassion can be accomplished in you.

December 7

CHURCH AND STATE

They are not to be separated, but to complement each other. Both the church and government are institutions given by God to men for their spiritual and physical well-being. Members of the true Church have been appointed by God to become the Bride of Christ. Government officials have been appointed by God to serve men here on earth. Both are accountable to God for their actions. So if the church and state fight each other, they are rebelling against God Himself and will be punished accordingly.

Romans 13:1-8; 1 Timothy 2:1-3; Titus 3:1-2; 1 Peter 2:13-17

- The church is to minister God's grace.
  The state is to administer justice.
- The church is to expose evil.
  The state is to restrain evil.
- The church is to carry out the Great Commission.
  The state is to guarantee the freedom to do so.
- The church must not use political power for spiritual values.
  The state must not use political power to attack spiritual values.
- The church must adhere to Judeo-Christian principles.
  The state must uphold Judeo-Christian principles.

December 8

GOING FULL CIRCLE

The average age of a civilization has been around 200 years. They go through these following stages -

From bondage to spiritual faith.
        From spiritual faith to great courage.
                From courage to liberty.
                        From liberty to abundance.
                                From abundance to selfishness.
                        From selfishness to complacency.
                From complacency to apathy.
        From apathy to dependency.
From dependency back to bondage.

December 9

HOW MUCH FAITH IS NEEDED?

A tiny seed of faith has enough power to defeat Satan, regardless of the size and nature of the problem. How can this power be triggered off? By *believing* that God is using the situation for our good. We then immediately experience the comfort of the Holy Spirit that says: "God is now in charge. He may or may not remove the problem, but He will sustain you."

If we are thankful for everything that is in our life, new things begin to happen. Joy and peace start to flow into our souls. This is God's gift to us for obeying His Word that says: "In everything give thanks, for this is the will of God in Christ Jesus."

We have to decide how to release this tiny spec of faith that is dormant within us. Each day presents numerous opportunities to say <u>YES</u> to Jesus, no matter what the circumstances are. We can learn to accept difficult situations as coming from God without giving Him a deadline to remove them.

Fasten your eyes on Jesus. Then remind yourself that in God's dimension of time <u>all</u> prayers are answered already. Then be happy for the opportunity to exercise your faith in the ongoing *NOW*.

True authority is a legal and rightful power given to us.
True submission is the voluntary act of committing ourselves to the will of someone else.
Resignation is surrender to somebody else at the expense of our own will.

December 10

A STAGEPLAY IN FOUR ACTS

ACT ONE
      Affirm your faith.
      Choose whether to follow the unredeemed or the Holy Spirit.
      Transfer the sealed decision to the will.

ACT TWO
      Abide in Christ.
      Commit yourself to fellowship (Enoch), obedience (Abraham), witness (Daniel).
      Trust in the Word.

ACT THREE
      Acknowledge the ways of the Lord.
      Comfort yourself in the Holy of Holies.
            Food (Manna), Water (Tablets of the law), Light (Lampstand),
            Air (Mercy Seat, God's approval), Protection (Cherubs).
      Thank and praise God for everything the way it is right now.

In case of failure -

ACT FOUR
      Admit your sins.
      Carry them to the Cross.
      Turn around and go back to the Father's House.

December 11

THREE PLACES TO GO

- *THE CRUCIFIED CHRIST.*
      Whatever is not pleasing to God must be carried to the Cross for crucifixion.

- *THE RISEN CHRIST.*
      Any work we have to do must be performed in the power of His resurrection.

- *THE GLORIFIED CHRIST.*
      Whatever is beyond our strength must be delegated to the glorified Christ.

The provisions of the Cross, the Resurrection and the Glorification are sufficient for all our needs. The first two are available for us in this life, the latter will be ours after the redemption is completely manifested. Until then, Christ will performs for us what we are not asked to do.

December 12

HARDSHIP AFTER SALVATION

To get the Israelites out of Egypt would have taken only a few days. But to take "Egypt" out of them took forty years. There was basic inactivity in the wilderness - no jobs, no responsibilities, no satisfaction for doing something worthwhile, no battles but no victories either, much boredom and tests of patience.

We may get weary <u>on</u> the way, but we should never get weary <u>of</u> the way. There is a supply for the needs of the weary ones, but nothing for the drop-outs. We are allowed times of ease while following the Lord, but we must never seek an easier way than God's way. Our own way leads to a dead end, so we have to go all the way back and start over.

In the Promised Land there is not a one time instant victory, but many slow and painful conquests. Satan's first priority is for us to violate God's will. In a confrontation with Satan, don't use God's Word, if you are not totally committed to it. Only when God's Word has become Life to you, it becomes death to Satan. The moment you declare : "God's Word says......", the enemy retorts: "Has God said?" At that moment, don't argue about who is right, <u>do</u> what you *know* is right. Don't argue about Truth, live it.

To yield to temptation is like "selling our birthright", that includes abiding in Christ and living on Holy Hill, for a "bowl of soup" with ingredients of guilt, regret and defeat.

December 13

ARE YOU WILLING ?

When headed in the wrong direction, you must be willing to make a U-turn.

- Are you willing to discard all knows sins like an old coat? Colossians 3:5-9
- Are you willing to put on a new spiritual self like a clean garment? Col 3:10-14
- Are you willing to give thanks and praise God for everything? Col 3:15
- Are you willing to abide by God's Word? Col 3:16
- Are you willing to put Christ first in any relationship? Col 3:17 – 4:1
- Are you willing to pray faithfully for any person? Col 4:2
- Are you willing to communicate God's grace to others with love? Col 4:6

God is the ever flowing wellspring of love and blessedness.
Christ is the reservoir to store the fullness of God.
The Holy Spirit is the stream of Living Water that flows to us.
We are the channels through which the love of God, the manifestations of Christ and the power of the Holy Spirit are brought to earth and imparted to others.
Psalm 104:10-13

December 14

BASIC NEEDS OF A HUSBAND

- He needs to be respected as a man and a leader. Look to him for protection, spiritual direction and financial provision.
- He needs to be built up in self-esteem. Praise him for who he is and express gratitude for what he does.
- He needs a pleasant atmosphere at home. Keep yourself well groomed and your house comfortable and clean.
- He needs forgiveness and support when making mistakes. Don't nag or complain. Never discuss his failures and weaknesses with others.
- He needs privacy and freedom. Try to accept and respect the basic differences of the physical, mental and spiritual needs between men and women.
- He needs a grateful and cheerful wife. Don't expect him to fulfill all your needs. Your happiness is an encouragement to him.
- He needs to be proud of his wife. Her reputation reflects directly on his leadership. She should be well spoken of by others.

December 15

BASIC NEEDS OF A WIFE

- She needs the stability and direction of a spiritual leader. Let her know that you are in continuous contact with the Lord.
- She needs to know that she is an equal partner and contributes to the well being of the family.
- She needs to be told often that she is loved and appreciated. Stand by her in failures and weaknesses with patience and encouragement.
- She needs security and protection. Be sensitive to her physical and emotional limitations. Provide loving, tactful but firm guidance.
- She needs to be understood. Take time to really get to know her intimately. Ask questions and be a good listener.
- She needs to know that she is a true friend. Share with her your ideas, plans, goals and dreams.
- She needs a husband to be proud of. Keep a neat, attractive appearance and display good manners and courtesy at all times.

December 16

CHAIN REACTION
1 Thessalonians 5:14-22

1) Warn those who are out of line.
2) Encourage the faint-hearted.
3) Support and protect the weak.
4) Be patient with everybody.
5) Never retaliate, but always show kindness.
6) Rejoice in who Christ is, what He has done, is doing now and is going to do.
7) Pray without ceasing. Keep communication lines open with God at all times.
8) In everything give thanks for the way things are right now and be content.
9) Quench not the Spirit. Be sensitive to the "Still Small Voice".
10) Obey what you know is the will of God.
11) Test everything and hold fast to what is good.
12) Abstain from all forms of evil.

If I violate 9, 10, 11 or 12, I cannot fulfill 6.
        Then it is impossible to obey 4 and 5.
                I have no right to do 1.
                        2 and 3 become unconvincing.
                                I am no longer able to do 8.
                                        My lifeline of 7 gets plugged up.

December 17

WHAT TO DO WITH THE BIBLE

To fully benefit from the Bible we must -

*   Read it. 2 Timothy 3:16
*   Bathe in it. John 15:3
*   Look into it. James 1:23-25
*   Study it. 2 Timothy 2:15; Hebrews 5:12-14
*   Meditate on it. Psalm 1:2; 1 Timothy 4:15
*   Memorize it. Deuteronomy 11:18; Psalm 119:11
*   Teach it. Deuteronomy 11:19
*   Talk about it. Psalm 51:13; Matthew 28:19-20

He is a fool who will not give what he cannot keep -
to gain what he cannot keep.

December 18

GUARD YOUR TREASURE
Matthew 7:6

"Do not give what is holy to the dogs, they will only turn and attack you."

As a born-again Christian, my life has become "holy" in a sense that now I am the Temple of the Holy Spirit who dwells in me. If my words and actions convey defeat, unforgiveness, ingratitude and self-pity, my Christian testimony is tarnished, God's faithfulness is questioned and Christianity made unappealing. The unbeliever will then attack and tear me apart.

"Do not throw your pearls in front of pigs, they will only trample them underfoot."

If I share with unbelievers things that are very precious to me, like my intimate relationship with the Father, Son and Holy Spirit and my insights from the Bible, they will misunderstand, ridicule, criticize and reject me.

December 19

WISDOM FROM THE PROVERBS

CHAPTER 3

Verse 3 - Keep a balance between mercy and truth.
"   5 - Trust God always.
"   6 - Acknowledge and accept God's sovereignty in everything.
"   7 - Cling to God and shun evil.
"   21 - Keep the teachings before you at all times.
"   22 - It is the secret for inner strength and outer beauty.
"   23 - Then you will not stumble into sin.
"   24 - There is nothing to fear.
"   25 - No sudden calamity will come upon you.
"   26 - The Lord Himself is your protection.
"   27 - Be a channel for God's blessings to others.

CHAPTER 4

Verse   4 - Obey and you will live.
"   20-22 - Keep His Word.
"   23 - Keep your thoughts pure.
"   24 - Don't tell any lies.
"   25 - Keep your eyes on the Lord.
"   26 - Make long-term goals and plan the details ahead.
"   27 - Stick to you vows and be aware of deceptions.

December 20

"PRAY WITHOUT CEASING"
1 Thessalonians 5:17

- *ATTENTION PRAYER* - Jeremiah 29:13; 33:3; John 14:23
  Tune in to God's sovereignty, holiness and love.
  Embrace Christ as sinbearer, advocate and friend.
  Turn to the Holy Spirit as teacher, supplier of strength and helper.

- *ATTITUDE PRAYER* - Romans 12:12
  Unbelief, pride and ingratitude conceived in the <u>mind</u> are contaminating the <u>emotions</u>. When sin enters the mind, obedience to the Word of God can activate the <u>will</u> to offer the sacrifice of praise that will diffuse the pent-up emotions.

- *ASSURANCE PRAYER* - Jeremiah 31:3; Rom 8:28; 2 Cor 12:9; Hebrews 13:5
  Meditate on, thank for and implement God's perfect love, infinite wisdom and absolute control.

- *ASSIGNMENT PRAYER* - Isaiah 6:8; Luke 1:38
  Report for duty and submit to whatever God asks.

- *ACTION PRAYER* - John 9:4; 1 Corinthians 3:6
  Faithfully do the task at hand with God's grace, Christ's encouragement and the Holy Spirit's strength.

- *ALTRUISM PRAYER* - Colossians 1:9-11
  For unbelievers : Conviction, confession, conversion, comprehension,
                       commitment, cover and comfort.
  For believers : Grace, joy, peace, contentment, guidance, courage and strength.

- *ADORATION PRAYER* - Psalm 103:2; Job 1:21; Psalm 150
  Thanksgiving for past blessings. Praise during the dark night of the soul or the present intense battle. Worship for who God IS.

December 21

PRESENTS FOR YOUR CHILDREN

- To lead them to Jesus. John 14:6
- To show them where to go during the storms of life. Psalm 46:1; Proverbs 14:26
- To teach them to view life from God's perspective. Isaiah 55:8-9
- To remind them that they are accountable to God for everything they do, even when
  no one is watching. Romans 14:12; 2 Corinthians 5:10

December 22

I CAN CHOOSE

It is up to me to live above my circumstances -

- I can choose to deal with my sin nature.
- I can choose to accept God's redemption through the Blood of Jesus Christ.
- I can choose to forgive all parties involved in causing me pain.
- I can choose to surrender all rights to be happy. Life is a boot camp for training, not a leisurely cruise.
- I can choose to accept the present assignment. Each person is given a unique way to serve God.
- I can choose to acknowledge that Jesus Christ, not I, is the center of the universe.
- I can choose to focus on Christ, not my circumstances.
- I can choose to trust the sovereignty of God and not fear the whims of man.
- I can choose to respond to hardships by drawing closer to God. Discouragement is replaced by greater intimacy with Him.
- I can choose to look at the Cross, knowing that God is in control of the worst tragedies.
- I can choose to see the broader picture, not just my personal problem.
- I can choose to reach out to others. Jesus did it on the Cross, we can do it too.

I may still face fierce opposition in the form of satanic attacks or divine chastisement. Job 1:19; Jeremiah 4:11-12; Jonah 4:8. But now I have access to the most powerful weapon there is - PRAISE. This weapon will not work for unbelievers, or for believers with unconfessed sins in their lives. Their "computer" freezes up, blocking any praise.

December 23

RICH YET HUMBLE

What is the abundant life? John 10:10

Worldly definition - Health, wealth, status, recognition, fame, power, good looks.
Spiritual definition - Freedom from guilt and penalty of sin, continuous access to the Trinity, assurance of God's grace, hope for eternal love, joy and peace in heaven.

Humility is perfect quietness of heart. It is to never be disturbed, distressed and irritated by trouble. It is to yield all rights and be content when ignored, blamed or despised. It is to dwell in the secret place of the Lord and be at peace in a deep sea of calmness, when there is turmoil all around. It is the Fruit of Christ's redemptive work on the Cross, manifested in those who are filled with the Holy Spirit.

December 24

A FORK IN THE ROAD

Shopping, decorating, partying, looking for the rotund man in a red suit ----------

But that is not where Jesus can be found.

Are you willing to wait quietly for a heavenly chorus proclaiming peace and goodwill towards men? Peace on earth does not mean absence of war, but peace with God by His provision of salvation. Goodwill means God's compassion and grace to all sinners.

So you decide to turn away from all the artificial glitter and ringing cash registers. Instead you follow a bright Star with your eyes, sublime music with your ears and a deep yearning in your heart. You are searching for a king in all of his splendor.

December 25

WRONG ADDRESS ?

Instead of a palace, you arrive at an overcrowded, filthy and smelly stable. There is a baby in a feed trough. The disappointment is so overwhelming that you hurry back to the politically correct world of materialism. Santa Claus will entertain the kids, and the spouse will get an electronic gadget or a trip to Las Vegas. At least it is clean here and smells nice.

But where is the love, joy and peace you so desperately crave? A baby in a dirty stable cannot possibly fill your needs. Or can he? Who is this baby? Where did he come from? Why is he here? How can he help me? What should be my response?

Don't switch on CNN for answers. Turn to the one and only true source of information to explain the mysteries of "who", "where", "why", "how" and "what" -

THE WORD OF GOD

December 26

WORD = CHRIST
John 1:1-5, 14

"From eternity past, there was, is and will be the Word, the Lord Jesus Christ. He was with God and He is God. Everything was created by the *SPOKEN WORD* and darkness had to flee at the command of the Light. The Word became a human being to lead us with loving-kindness to the Way, the Truth and the eternal Life."

The LIVING WORD sits at the right hand of the Father
and interprets the WRITTEN WORD for us through the Holy Spirit.

December 27

FROM FAITH TO LOVE
2 Peter 1:5-7

- *FAITH* - It originates in the spirit and permeates the soul (mind, will, emotions). Salvation means being born again and filled with the Holy Spirit.
- *VIRTUE* - Separation from evil thoughts, words and deeds. A deliberate turning towards the Light. Burial of the old self, resurrection to the new life.
- *KNOWLEDGE* - Searching out God's Word for instruction and understanding.
- *SELF-CONTROL* - Turning the knowledge into action. Laying up treasures in heaven for eternal values. Learning to put aside personal desires.
- *PATIENCE* - Endurance, suffering, steadfastness, unwavering commitment.
- *GODLINESS* - Spiritual maturity, humility, Christ-likeness. Responding to everything with faith, trust, praise, joy and peace.
- *BROTHERLY KINDNESS* - Human affection, forgiveness, encouragement, understanding, empathy. We exercise brotherly kindness by giving out what we have received from the Lord.
- *LOVE* - Agape. Unconditional love, no strings attached, compassion. It is a gift of grace and a Fruit of the Holy Spirit. We can only be channels for this love until we are completely conformed to the image of Christ.

December 28

OPEN LINES TO GOD

To be filled with the Holy Spirit is like a hose being filled with water. Turning on the tap is our surrender to Christ, confession of our sins and acceptance of God's forgiveness. Without turning on the tap, the hose remains empty. If anything comes between God and us, the hose gets plugged up, and then contains stagnant water that turns foul and stinky. That is why "plugged-up" Christians are more offensive than "empty" people.

Being filled with the Spirit is not a one-time experience, but an ongoing process. We have to keep the hose open to the flow by continuously confessing our failures and accepting God's forgiveness. Branches cannot grow and produce fruit without the life-giving sap flowing through them from the vine at all times.

To determine what blocks the life-line of the Holy Spirit, we have to ask -

- Is there anyone I won't forgive?
- Is there anything I won't give up for God?
- Is there anything I won't thank God for?

December 29

WORTH REMEMBERING

The first and second law of Thermodynamics deal with the energy exchange in the universe. Any theory about the origin of the universe must not violate these laws.

FIRST LAW - Energy cannot be created or destroyed. The sum total of energy never changes. The quantity is forever fixed and does not increase or decrease.
SECOND LAW - Each time an energy exchange takes place, a portion of the original energy goes into a less useful form.

Therefore, the state of our universe is one of quantitative stability and qualitative decay.
The second law of Thermodynamics is a consequence of Adam's sin.

"Christ showed His love by dying for us. We show our love by living for Him."

"Those who see God's hand in everything, can best leave everything in God's hand."

"Pain is inevitable - misery is optional."

"The only thing we have ever learned from history is -
                    that we have never learned anything from history."

December 30

ENLISTING AS A SOLDIER FOR CHRIST

- *THE REQUIREMENTS* - Luke 9:23 "If you want to follow me, you have to deny yourself (give up the desire to be somebody, accepted and at ease), and pick up your cross (to suffer for Jesus, be maligned and rejected)."
- *REPORTING FOR DUTY* - Romans 12:12 "Let hope keep you joyful. Let love give you strength in afflictions. Let faith keep you in prayer."
- *CLASSROOM INSTRUCTION* - Learning the plans, strategies and weapons for the spiritual warfare. The textbook is the Bible, the teacher the Holy Spirit.
- *TRAINING EXERCISES* - Meeting daily challenges by applying what was learned and rehearsing for the real battle.
- *ACTUAL COMBAT* - Are you prepared for the real test?
- *EVALUATING THE REPORT CARD* - Grades A to F.
- *STEPS TO TAKE WHEN WOUNDED IN THE WAR* -
    - Confess your sins and mistakes.
    - Forgive the ones who hurt you.
    - Pray for their salvation.
    - Review and memorize your curriculum.

December 31

THANKING GOD

Remember to *always* be thankful for -

- Past blessings.
    1 Samuel 7:12; 12:24; Psalm 103:1-2

- The way things are.
    Psalm 34:1; Ephesians 5:20; 1 Thessalonians 5:18; Hebrews 13:15

- Promises from the Word.
    Deuteronomy 31:8; Isaiah 41:10, 13; John 14:1-3; Romans 8:28-39

- Uncertainty.
    Isaiah 55:8-9; Jeremiah 29:11; 2 Corinthians 2:5; Hebrews 11:1

- Opportunity to grow.
    Psalm 119:67, 71; James 1:2-4; 1 Peter 1:6-8

- New beginnings.
    Psalm 118:24; Lamentations 3:22-23; 2 Corinthians 5:17; Philippians 3:13-14

- Ultimate victory.
    Isaiah 65:17; John 16:33; 1 Corinthians 2:9; 1 John 5:4; Revelation 21:4-7

"GLORY TO GOD IN THE HIGHEST"

A M E N